Love and Relationship
How To
AVOID
MARRYING A TOAD!!

JOHN JOHNSTON

LOVE AND RELATIONSHIP

HOW TO AVOID MARRYING A TOAD!!

Copyright © 2011 by John Johnston

ISBN: 978-0-98274-671-4
Library of Congress Number: 2011925338

Edited by Judy Ray Johnston

Formatting and Proofreading by
Cris Wanzer/MANUSCRIPTS TO GO (spuntales@gmail.com)

Published by Dark Planet Publishing
www.darkplanetpublishing.com
For volume sales call 760-747-2734

Dedicated

To

Judy Ray Johnston

and

To Every Broken Heart

That Still Has the Courage

To Quest for Love's Fulfillment

"You've got to have a dream!
If you don't have a dream,
How you gonna have a dream come true?"
From Rodgers & Hammerstein's *South Pacific*

Contents

Chapter 1
Toads!

Ah, spring! Love is in the air and nature's beauty beckons.

Georgie blinks his big brown eyes in wonder and high expectation as he tries to clear the last of the winter's mud away from the entrance to his humble little abode.

All the RSVPs have come back and absolutely everybody's going to be there!

"I'm really nervous, but I'm also incredibly happy...and out of my mind excited!" he shouts out loud. *"But arranged marriages, I wonder who invented that? Well, they say in India they really work well. Something about having your astrology chart done to find the right match. But this isn't India. This is heartland. This is Indiana! No time to think about that right now. I've got to get dressed and get down to the pond."*

Outdoor weddings are definitely in this spring. Georgie arrives early, and already the place is hopping. Lavish platters are piled high with exotic bugs. All his best buddies are there with their new brides. It's a glorious day for nuptials.

"There she is! Wow, what a dress. It's gorgeous! I wonder what she really looks like under that veil? Well, I'll soon find out!"

The old minister hops down the aisle and takes out his holy text. Right on cue the little bluebirds begin to sing. And at last the long awaited moment has arrived.

"She's walking right toward me!" And with his heart pounding, Georgie hears through the emotional haze words about love and loyalty, and then hears himself saying, *"I do."*

The old minister then looks up, smiles and says, *"And now, you may kiss your bride."*

Georgie steps forward and lifts back his new bride's veil and looks lovingly and expectantly into her big dark eyes. Then his mind screams in terror. *"Oh No! She's a toad!"*

But just like in ponds and meadows all over Indiana, and in India, too, for that matter, toads *always* marry other toads. Of course, that's what Georgie is, too! So, that's the point. Like draws like. And that's exactly the way it works in relationship.

You draw someone in relationship at your own level of woundedness. Or, stated another

John Johnston

way, you draw someone in relationship that matches your psychological, emotional and spiritual level of development.

Although, it doesn't always seem that way! Often our souls draw seeming opposites as a way of creating learning that can help us move toward eventual wholeness. The two sides of this coin are really *one* coin. They just look entirely different. A wounded abuser draws a wounded soul with a matching victim's consciousness. Therefore, the more complete and whole we are individually, the more complete and whole will be our partner. And that's what we're striving to become through the process of relationship.

So, there's the fundamental truth that shines its light in the direction *you* need to go in order to have the self-discovery, self-healing, and self-transformation that will, at last, fulfill your longing for a healthy, intimate, joyous and love saturated relationship.

Therefore, I boldly say that this little book *can* change your life. Not because it's *my* book, but because it is based upon universal truth and universal laws which come from the All-Knowing Benevolent Source of our universe. And just like gravity, whether you believe it or not isn't the issue — its laws and structures apply to us all regardless, all the time and without exception.

3

The key element to whether this book will be helpful to you or not will be determined by your own free will choices to apply the higher principles I'll be offering you. I know, without doubt, that if you'll make a conscientious effort to apply these principles you *will* be able to change your consciousness; and in so doing, be able to draw to yourself the wonderful and fulfilling relationship that you're seeking. In the process, you will also uncover a deeper, more authentic sense of who you really are.

You and I are fortunate to be living at a very special time. One that is now ripe with fresh opportunity for both personal and spiritual rediscovery. We have all come into this world to improve and reform our understanding of how life works. We then practice putting the new understandings we gain to work in the crucible of our daily lives in order to prove or disprove their relative value in bringing us increasing joy, wisdom and contentment.

When we start to understand how we actually create the conditions of our lives through the all-powerful forces of our thoughts, desires, and willpower, we can then begin to consciously *restructure* our thoughts and desires so they will begin to guide us more successfully toward what is best for us in every situation.

By learning to apply the universal principles I'm going to share with you, you will not only become more successful in relationship, but you will significantly progress in the advancement of other essential character traits. Traits like unconditional love, patience, inclusiveness, courage, wisdom, forgiveness, compassion, and service to the greater good.

When you take this high road, the conscious, soul guided road, you will accelerate your assimilation of even greater gifts of love and wisdom that you will find continually flowing to you through the interactive nature of relationship.

Here even higher levels of intimacy can be achieved that bring sharing, caring, loving, and unconditional trust and support that make the angels catch their breath. In a word, it becomes holy. These are the lofty regions where two egos are not as much in relationship as are two souls.

All of this and more can be gained through the highest expressions of relationship; and therefore, the *potential* of relationship offers you one of the most rewarding journeys you will ever take. Absolutely everything you are seeking awaits you. You need only uncover what the variables are in order to begin creating new thought patterns and their resultant actions that together will remodel your consciousness and consequently, your life!

In this way, you will find that you can begin to dramatically reform your life from the inside out; which is the only true way to achieve a lasting self-transformation. A transformation that will lead you to a fuller and more authentic expression of who you really are — a joyous and rapidly evolving soul, someone who has two unique gifts to give in this world: one, through your service to the greater world family, and the other in the intimate sanctuary of relationship.

To get to where you really want to go requires us to light the way with truth. There is no other way. Without a total commitment to truth, honesty, and self-discovery, you'll end up following many a false map scribbled by your ego's illusions; illusions that will only deliver you to the land of increasing ignorance, confusion, disappointment, and pain. And, I can tell you firsthand that this land is far more than a geographic metaphor, for I was long a self-imposed prisoner on those isles of self-deception. The good news is that even pain can be appreciated if it helps you learn the lessons that it offers.

My hope in offering you this book is that it will encourage you to be wiser than I was by putting these truths to work in your life *now,* while your heart and mind are receptive. If you do, you'll immediately intuit a joyous roar of approval welling up from within as all your angels jump to their feet to cheer you on your way!

One more thing before we begin. If you happen to be a dominantly linear personality, you're in for a consciousness-expanding ride. For the road to a healthy and idyllic relationship is not a road that goes straight from point A to point B. Rather, it's a journey that will lead you in many different directions, often at the same time.

Here's a metaphor that will paint a picture for you of what I mean. Imagine that your consciousness is represented by an infinite dark wall. Each time you gain some new understanding, you create a window in that wall where the light of your new insight pours through. As you begin to create more and more portals into the unknown, you not only get more individual pieces of understanding, but you also, like a mosaic, gradually begin to see and understand the larger picture to which all the individual pieces contribute.

In this way I'll be focusing on creating and expanding several different *openings in the wall* of your consciousness with the intent that, by the end of our journey together, you'll have a more complete and soul-empowering vision of what the greatest relationships can be and how you can actually integrate this vision into *your* life in order to experience its great abundance of love and joy.

To create this larger canvas for you, I'll be using lots of stories and metaphors to give you insights and pictures that will more easily engage your feeling nature and stimulate your intuition, which alone can take you to those farther horizons where you will be better able to look out upon your soul's unfettered potential in wordless awe and wonder.

Chapter 2
Your Relationship With Yourself

The initial key that you need to bring to this process is the understanding that the progress you want to make in having a healthier relationship starts *within yourself*, and not with your outer circumstances or other people. And a problem correctly defined is a problem half solved!

By understanding that our lives are built out of our thoughts and feelings and the actions they generate, we can see clearly where we need to start. Introspection, yoga, prayer, meditation, self-analysis, affirmations, and visualization all show us that the way to personal problem solving begins on the inside.

Our understanding of the exciting and rewarding world of both personal and interpersonal growth is rapidly expanding. And much of that expansion is because we are now paying more attention to the "what" and "why" of our thoughts and feelings. By paying attention to what we are thinking and feeling, it becomes easier for us to see whether we're going in a direction that benefits us. So, we need to be regularly asking ourselves questions like, *"Is my life moving in ways that are truly taking me forward and making me happier, or not?"*

More and more science is confirming that the world, yours, mine and everyone's, is built out of the fabric of our thoughts.* And in that special area of our world that we call "Relationship" it, too, all begins with the patterns of the thoughts we create and concentrate upon. It all begins with what you first think and feel in the womb of your own consciousness

It is here, within your own mind, that you have already created your *half* of a relationship package. That is to say, you have already created the magnetic ego-personality entity that you call "Me." Therefore, unless you make changes in who you are at the foundational level of your thoughts and feelings, you are not going to be able to change the patterns that dominate your relationships.

Consequently, it follows that the initial and most primal relationship you need to focus on is the one that you have with yourself. With that understood, it should be easier to accept that as a

---

* Wall Street Journal Article 2002 *By Sharon Begley: Latest Research in Brain Plasticity Suggests Potential for Continuous Brain Development Throughout Life* *"The brain also remakes itself based on something much more ephemeral than what we do: It rewires itself based on what we think."*

unique bundle of thoughts, feelings, beliefs, prejudices, likes and dislikes, you naturally draw people into your life that match your "bundle."

One way to look at it is to imagine yourself as a magnet; a magnet that has its own unique "DNA"-like configuration. If you've become unhappy with the results of your relationship experiences so far, do you think that things will improve just because you want them to? The answer, of course, is no. But that *is* the first step! The critical second step is you have to change your energetic "DNA," because if you don't change your "bundle" then you will continue to draw yourself right back into the same set of variables!

Simply put, you have to change yourself, and that begins by changing your thinking, because your life is the product of the patterns of your thoughts. Dr. Wayne Dyer distills this for us in his wonderful book, *The Power of Intention*, when he explains to us what the science of *quantum physics* now proves. Which is: *"When you change the way you look at things, the things you look at change!"*

This is far more than just a warm and fuzzy esoteric statement. It is, in fact, the quantifiable and scientifically proven workings of our universe. Therefore, this is the law that *you* will need to work with in order to fulfill each and every dream that is in your heart.

Chapter 3
Woundedness

From those who have already begun this journey we learn that, *"You draw someone in relationship at your own level of woundedness."* The first time someone shared that thought with me my mouth dropped open. *Of course!* I thought. It was completely obvious, once I looked at it that way.

What we are automatically reflects back to us from the mirror of our life's interactions with others. Can you see the beauty in that? If you make the effort to improve yourself, if you remodel your consciousness, you will draw both new friends and a life partner that match your new level of spiritual and emotional strength and understanding. What a liberating insight that is, when you discover this aspect of your personal power and then use it to positively redirect your life. It absolutely is you who is in the driver's seat.

So, let's drop that old false paradigm of *victim consciousness*! It's a hangover from the dark ages when the collective consciousness of mankind was so clouded and dense that people, in general, knew nothing of energy, electricity or the creative power of the mind and the will. Fortunately, this is now a rapidly evolving *new* age powered by more enlightened thought and deeper spiritual perception.

Even our old friend, Albert Einstein, affirms this core truth as regards the power of the mind when he tells us, "Think you can or think you can't. Either way, you're right!" And from another eternal friend we hear a stunning truth that stirs our souls. "Know ye not that ye are gods?"*

Yes, we have all been deluded into drinking from the dark cup of mortal illusions, and for a long time we've thought that joy and unbroken happiness can never be ours. But the truth is they are *already* ours! We have only to rediscover them.

Finding that you have the power to both alter and dramatically improve all your relationships is a valuable piece in helping you rediscover who and what you really are. When you consciously acknowledge this truth, it will bring in a great ray of understanding and empowerment because it will immediately lift from your consciousness the delusion that your life's challenges are someone else's fault.

This permanently removes the debilitating,

* 1 Corinthians 3:16

limiting, and deluding drug of *"victim consciousness."* In doing so, you simultaneously step up to a new and healthier level of self-perception and self-empowerment. This, then, is the beginning of up-leveling your consciousness and your relationships, and will automatically put you more in alignment with Truth. This is huge, because real power and lasting happiness cannot be accessed outside of being in alignment with Truth.

Of course, this has an energetic component, as well. Everything is based in energy, so the purer your consciousness and the more aligned with Truth that you are, the more powerful, magnetic and joyous you will become, because Truth, Love, and Joy are all aspects of the Omnipotent Creator, and therefore are inherent in you, as well.

From here it's crystal clear as to *who* needs to change their thought patterns, their life and their relationship patterns. So, repeat after me: *"ME!"* Great! Just that quickly you've already begun! *"For with Willingness, all things are possible!"*

Love and Relationship

Chapter 4
Broken Hearts

When you put your tender heart out into the arena of human love there is always risk. Your heart can be ignored, cheated against, lied to, manipulated, abused, dropped on the rocks of pain, stomped on, replaced by someone new, and lots of other horror stories. Each of you could add to this list, no doubt. Not everyone finds their true love the first time out. Perhaps you noticed!

All universal structures, including relationships, are built upon foundations of law. Life has rules! To ignore them is to put yourself in serious peril. Whether it's the material, the mental, the emotional, or the spiritual, everything in creation has been designed by the Divine Intelligence to guide you on your way.

It is our Spirit assigned challenge, as soul expressions of our Benevolent Source, that we courageously take up the quest to unravel the great mysteries of the universe, and to discover and reclaim the greatest treasure of all, the awareness of our own Divine nature.

One of the largest diamonds in this treasure chest of Self-discovery is uncovering the beauty and value of relationship when it is experienced in its highest expressions. And then, like diamonds that are uncorrupted across the ages, relationships that are based in *Divine Love* bring unbounded joy and fulfillment and last far beyond the grave. So, pick up the shovels of your enthusiasm and willingness and let's get to work, for your treasure is eager to be discovered!

As with all the other journeys we take in life, this one needs to start from where you are right now. And for most of us that is from the recovery house of a bruised or broken heart.

Through metaphors and stories I offer you ideas and pictures that more easily engage your feeling nature, your heart, than if I were to just speak to your mental and reasoning nature only. And when we're talking about relationship, while I need to speak to both your head and your heart, the deeper truth is that I need to talk to your heart significantly more. Successful relationships are dominantly experienced on a non-verbal level. It's about having a natural intuitive awareness of your partner's mental, emotional, and spiritual status. This doesn't mean you won't have meaningful and wonderful conversations that run way into the wee hours!

What's useful to point out here is that the intuitive and feeling nature needs to be engaged first in order to evolve a relationship to increasingly higher levels. It is foundational, and you won't progress very far without it. If you are trying to connect with other people (whether it be an individual or a group) just with your intellect and ideas, you won't be as fully successful as those who connect with people on a feeling level first.

There's an old salesman's saying that is right on the mark. It says, *"People need to know you care, before they care to know."* And I can speak to this firsthand from having had many years of experience teaching and speaking with individuals and groups of all ages and backgrounds.

Through the years I have become a far more successful communicator, and far better at developing meaningful relationships, after learning to connect with people first on a feeling level; genuinely expressing love, caring, enthusiastic interest and compassion before attempting to move on to whatever content I was there to share.

And if my experience doesn't fully convince you to lead with your heart instead of your head, then I'd suggest you just watch the news! Our collective consciousness in this world is in a severely toxic state because we are completely out of balance. Not just with nature, but more fundamentally, we are out of balance within our own consciousness.

Amazingly, the remedy is not all that difficult to understand or to accomplish. It begins and is accomplished when we learn to be in an equal and harmonious *relationship* between our own hearts and our own minds, between our reason and our feeling, right within ourselves. So, it isn't all about this "tired old world" or our partner who needs to change. It's about you and I being the change we want to see in the world.

The deeper truth is that it's about you and me healing our bruised and broken hearts by using the God-given tools of positive introspection and meditation that lead us to the awareness and guidance of the indwelling Spirit that has become each and every one of us. When you begin to make that connection in the living stillness within, you will have begun the development of the inner *Divine Relationship,* where you'll automatically discover a joyous and powerful increase in your own sense of personal value and purpose. This is the most powerful way to heal a broken heart, and the most direct! And it is the only healing of the heart that is permanent.

You know why that is? It is because the degree to which you are aware of your soul's true nature of love and joy is equal to the degree to which you are free from the pain of loss and suffering that is inherent in this ever-changing world. By accessing this deeper awareness of your Higher Self, you will find that you are living on a higher plane of consciousness. And the higher the plane, the more joy and love you will experience.

When you start to tap into the ocean of joy that is right within yourself, the *outer* conditions that brought on your depression or sense of loss begin to lose their power over you. These are the utterly priceless fruits of creating an interior life. And there are none sweeter anywhere in this world than those that come directly from within yourself.

This is exactly the process that can get you *out* of a toxic or abusive relationship and into a healthier and more joyous one! Like attracts like, and it is the unequivocal truth that if you change your consciousness sufficiently, universal forces, by law, will respond and create new circumstances that will free you from a relationship that is no longer an energetic match.

There's a bonus, too. In doing so, you'll also be giving a gift through your example that others will be inspired to follow. This is the way the world will really recover from its broken *relationship* with truth. Our world family will begin to accelerate this recovery when more and more people like you start making the effort to up-level their emotional and spiritual health and understanding.

The good news is, this has *already* begun! And *you* have an important part to play in that healing change! There is no soul who is not destined for fulfillment and enlightenment. It is only about *when* you're going to exercise your wisdom-guided free will and begin. The fact that you're reading this book suggests to me that your time is NOW!

So, as you begin to awaken to a deeper and more conscious awareness of your soul's great power and purpose, you automatically begin to feel increasing amounts of joy and contentment. And learning how to listen to and understand your feelings is a critical component in your soul's evolutionary journey, not only as it applies to relationship, but in every aspect of your treasured life.

Chapter 5
Feelings

While we're on the subject of feelings, let's get a deeper handle on their positive and negative aspects. We've all seen that visual of an angel on one shoulder and a devil on the other, but for me it wasn't until I upgraded my understanding of what that was really all about that I discovered one of the most powerful and freeing tools in my self-transformation kit.

As every scripture and every saint across the ages has pointed out, there are two forces battling it out here in creation, the positive force that leads us back toward Spirit, and the negative force that pulls us toward matter. And their characteristics are clear.

The dark force strives to lead us into the delusiveness of matter by encouraging us to seek our happiness solely through the senses, through exclusiveness, and through a separate sense of ego-self. Spirit pulls at our consciousness by encouraging us to respond to life's challenges with love, patience, wisdom, forgiveness, and inclusiveness, and by recognizing that we are all connected.

For me, that took on a more powerful and

rewarding context when I realized that the negative thoughts and feelings that I would have were *not* really my own creation! Of course, we all have the free will to entertain any thoughts we like, and we automatically access the cause and effect consequences of those choices. But, it's critically important to understand that *there are no original thoughts* in creation! Every positive and every negative thought already exists, and it is we who choose to access them by the ignorant or wise patterns of our choices, desires, and habits in life.

So, instead of feeling guilty or bad whenever a negative thought or feeling comes into my consciousness, like I used to, what I do now is immediately acknowledge that *"that's not me!"* or *"I'm not that."* As soon as I started doing this, I knew I was onto something really special, because my moodiness was dropping away so easily and unexpectedly!

Even though I'd forget about it once in a while in the beginning, whenever I'd remember it I'd redouble my efforts and keep doing it. After a few days of making the effort to keep practicing this consistently, these patterns gradually started to become a more dependable part of my consciousness. And now I have a very empowering new technique and habit.

With practice you'll discover, as I have, that you can consistently counteract and avoid moods, depression, and negative thoughts and feelings through this simple, but powerful and transformative practice. I believe the reason that it is so powerful is because, again, it deals directly with Truth — the Truth that we are *not* these negative thoughts and feelings. We are, in fact, the ever-joyous soul.

What's so wonderful is to recognize that there's nothing more to it than making conscious choices. And through our repeated choices of aligning ourselves with Truth, we create our new and valuable habits, which in time create our new and rewarding destiny. So, we have here an opportunity to create a new and more satisfying destiny by consciously creating new patterns of responses to the negative forces that want you to believe that *they* are you. They are not. They absolutely are not!

Through this recognition and practice we can learn to pull the energetic plug on "guilt." And when we do, one of the dark side's most powerful weapons instantly falls to the ground dead and is unable to touch you.

I tell you sincerely, this has been one of the greatest life changers for me. It's as if I have this esoteric light saber that, with one swing, I destroy the Darth Vader villain that's trying to invade my consciousness.

And because there's already enough pain in this world without extra servings of guilt served up on our plates each day, this is a wonderful and simple tool that anyone can use to re-empower their true sense of Self. So try it. It's nothing more than creating a simple new habit.

Of course, this is only one example of the powerful positive changes that anyone can make when they combine wisdom with the desire for self-improvement. The effects of such changes can bring you tremendous upgrades in your ability to stay unconditionally happy and in your sense of personal power. This increased happiness in your life can give you the extra power you need to overcome even greater obstacles, and help you in accomplishing all your worthy goals and ambitions. So, "Roll up your sleeves and get after it." For success and joy are the natural results that come to the spiritually ambitious!

There's a wonderful old Native American tale that illustrates this same principle in the battle between the forces of light and dark within our consciousness. It goes like this: A wise old grandfather explains to his young grandson that within every person there are two wolves that are constantly fighting. One wolf is positive and fights for what is good in life, and the other wolf is negative and strives to destroy the good wolf. After some reflection the young boy asks, "Which one wins, grandfather?" The grandfather replies, "The one that you feed."

So, by understanding that *you* did not create the negative wolf, and therefore you don't have to identify yourself with it or feed it with your guilt, you can instead "pull its plug" by not giving it any energy and by not buying into any guilt about it. And therefore, as one saint wisely pointed out, "An unrecognized visitor soon flees!"[*]

Visualization and Affirmation

Here's a visualization and affirmation for use with this technique.

Part One:

Whenever you recognize a negative thought or feeling coming into your consciousness, say, "That's not me," or "I'm not that," and visualize whatever that thought or feeling is instantly falling dead on the ground next to you.

---

[*] Swami Sri Yukteswar

Part Two:

Though it is wonderfully freeing to affirm what you are not, it is equally valuable to then affirm what you *are*. So, affirm things like this. "I am love, I am light, I am boundless compassion."

These are just my examples, of course. You should pick qualities or thoughts that resonate the most deeply for you. You need to discover what aspects of your soul's nature are most meaningful and affirming to you. And, over time, that becomes both clearer and easier to do as you deepen your interior life.

A Visualization Experience

Vacationing alone in France in 2001, my future wife had a significant personal shift. She said she could now see herself being married again. For over twenty years she'd been single; working on her own personal growth journey, creating a successful business, and living a useful and rewarding life as a single woman. Prior to this she said that she could not and did not envision herself ever being married again.

What shifted for her? That new vision didn't come out of nothingness, nor was it accidental. There are no accidents in our universe! The new "vision" came from her evolving self.

This new vision of herself co-created the new life elements appropriate for the new Judy. Perhaps not all on the conscious level, but perfect elements, nonetheless. The key point is that because she had done lots of personal growth work, some by choice and some delivered from outside her conscious choosing, this made her ready and open to receive this life-altering shift.

Let's put this key point in generic terms:

A new "vision" for your life comes from your evolving self, which then helps you co-create the new life elements appropriate for the fulfillment of your desires.

And you can accelerate this process by making an effort to do this consciously. Can you see now how important it is to *prepare* yourself for what you want?

You may want to be an NFL quarterback, for example, but unless you study football, develop you body, go to summer training camps, get on high school and college teams, do what you need to do in order to excel, and *"see yourself"* leading the team down the field for the winning touchdown with less than two minutes to go, like great quarterbacks do, you're going to end up watching the games on TV like the rest of us.

It's the same with relationship. Are you

working at making yourself into the kind of person you need to be in order to have the relationship you desire?   Can you "see and feel" yourself married to that partner of your dreams? Can you "see and feel" yourself enjoying each other's company?   Can you "see and feel" yourself treating and trusting your partner, lover and spouse as an absolute equal?   Is that a joyous feeling?   Can you "see and feel" yourself being safe, honored, trusted, loved, and appreciated as much as you desire to be for the rest of your life? Can you "see and feel" yourself being treated as an equal? Can you believe you deserve all this?

If you can answer all these questions with an enthusiastic "YES!" you've already gone a long way toward creating an ideal environment in your consciousness for the fulfillment of your desire. Further, do you spend more of your time enjoying and imagining your vision-desire for this relationship than you spend time and energy focusing on what you don't have in your life?   If you do, you should probably start making some room in your closet, because someone special is probably headed your way!   This is an example of how you can accelerate your dreams coming into reality.

If you're not quite there yet, you're like most of us, and I totally understand.   That is, in fact, exactly why I've written this book, so that you will be able to have a clearer understanding of the variables that will change your dreams into the actual experience you're seeking.

And what are these variables that will make the cosmic wheels turn in order for you to accomplish your intentions?   One is a strong mental and emotional picture of what you want, and the second is consistently keeping your attention and enthusiasm on what you want, rather than on what is missing.   And the third, and most important, is to up-level your consciousness.

So, along with building your interior life by adding a daily meditation practice to your life, I encourage you to start thinking about what this special relationship feels and looks like, even smells like. Start visualizing now about what it will be like to be with your ideal person. Imagine how you want to feel and behave in different settings with her or him.   What do you want it to look and feel like on work days, on weekends, on vacations, on birthdays, when you're with relatives and friends, when one of you is away on business, then sharing your experiences when you get back together?   How will you dialog about your differences? Visualize how you respectfully honor each other's various needs, and on and on.   See

31

what I mean? Really get into it. Then keep making it better, safer, and more intimate. But most of all, make it right for you.

This is not my vision, or your hairdresser's, or any other confidant's. Remember also; don't judge it as good or bad. Rather, just pay attention to what your thoughts and feelings are about it. In this way you can let your vision evolve without the unwelcome attention from some inner critic constantly throwing negatives at you. You'll naturally feel what's good for you and what's not, and you'll change and refine your thoughts and "visuals" as you begin to spend more and more time with them in the quiet sanctuary of your own heart and mind. It's a process and a journey. Give yourself permission to explore, to play, to create and evolve in your own inner workshop of co-creating.

Though you have yet to manifest your ideal relationship, you have visualized and created lots and lots of other things on your journey to today. If you're like most of us, you've done it with less than full awareness. Perhaps you got exactly what you were wishing for on your birthday or for Christmas. Maybe you got the new job you were excited about getting, or tickets to the big game, or the teacher you wanted.

I bet you also got some things you really,

really didn't want, too! You really didn't want your parents to find out about...but they did! You really didn't want to catch a cold from...but you did. It all seems so natural, and it is. But what you probably missed was that *you* were the one who created the outcome for these results through your own prior thoughts, feelings and actions!

The cutting-edge understanding today is that there are no accidents, and it is our own thoughts and feelings that create the fabric of our experiences. Actually, this is the best possible news. Not when looking backwards to the suffering that mankind has ignorantly brought upon itself in the past, but by looking forward to the new and better world that we can create right now, one person and one thought at a time.

Chapter 6
The Ostrich

Ostriches are the most amazing creatures. They're the largest flightless birds in the world and have a top running speed of about 45 mph. They also lay the largest eggs of any living bird species. If one of them ever kicked you, you'd probably sail into the next county. So, what do ostriches have to do with human relationships? Directly? Nothing. But by their example, a lot.

You remember the old adage about not putting your head in the sand like ostriches do, don't you? Well, that's exactly what you want to avoid when life is asking you to step up to the next level by doing the work you need to do to become a new and better person. This is exactly what life *is* asking of you in order to help you fulfill your desire for a healthier and more rewarding relationship.

But, as so often happens at this point, the dark side steps in with its greatest weapon, fear, frightens the heck out of us, and we run away. So, I thought I'd better tell you a couple of "run away" stories, lest you think that running away is the answer, because I've learned firsthand, it isn't!

Let's start you out first with a question. Do

you believe in miracles? I do. How about accidents? Do you believe in accidents? Nope, I don't.

I've come to understand that that's not the way the universe works. Rather, I've found that everything happens out of the cause and effect factory of the thoughts, desires, and actions that we all create in our lives. So, even the most horrible events and so-called accidents have an energetic beginning in our consciousness, either individually or collectively. It is out of our minds, and then with the responses of our emotions and the choices we make, that we create both our experiences and our destinies.

In my early years I was a musician. And for a time I studied French horn with a wonderful man by the name of Ralph Pyle, a long-time member of the Los Angeles Philharmonic Orchestra. One sunny afternoon in his Pasadena home, Ralph told me one of the most amazing stories I have ever heard. When Ralph was a young man he had a friend who had a strong premonition about his own death. So powerful was this feeling that his friend took his young wife and new baby up into the high Sierras and began building a home for them in a cave. During the construction, his wife and baby stayed in a nearby village, where he would come regularly whenever he needed supplies.

When one day he didn't come down as expected, the local people went up to check on him. They found him there lying in front of the cave, dead. A large bolt had fallen off an airplane and gone straight through his head.

Four years after Ralph told me this story, I found myself in the 25th Infantry Division in Chu Chi Vietnam. And though the fuller account will have to wait for a different venue, the salient point is that I was running across an open field straight into enemy automatic weapon fire. It was like playing cowboys and Indians when we were little kids. Only this time the bullets were real and whizzing just past my ears. Well, as it turned out, I made it all the way across the field completely untouched.

A few months later a friend of mine, a drummer in the 25th Infantry Division's band, was killed while the band was playing a concert in the division's recreation room, of all places!

There's another true story of a man who saw the world heading toward the Second World War. So, he decided to move someplace where the coming World War would never touch him and his family. After much study, he sold his home and moved his family to a tiny South Pacific island. Its name was Guadalcanal, where just a couple of years later over 25,000 Americans and Japanese lost their lives in some of the most horrific fighting of the entire war.

Were the results of any of those real events accidents? No, they were not. What I want you to understand is that we come and go from this world at exactly the moment when it is *best* for us to transition from one realm to another, regardless of the pleas or howls of our egos. So, if birth and death in this realm are the necessary entrance and exit points from the ever-changing schoolhouse of life, then doesn't it make better sense to trust that the Director of this cosmic show knows what She's doing, and that She has your best interests at heart, even if your limited, rational mind cannot understand it?

Therefore, if you're courageous enough and wise enough to accept and work with whatever life is offering you, you will surely progress more rapidly and with less pain than if you are constantly in a state of fear and avoidance. And I know about this principle firsthand. No matter how far or how fast you run away from what life is asking of you, when you arrive at your next hideout you'll be shocked to discover that the conditions that you are running away from are waiting there, with reinforcements, to greet you once again!

Perhaps this next story will underline this point for you. It shows us that if we keep on refusing life's encouragements to make an effort to improve ourselves, we'll eventually get a visit from *The Last Teacher.*

Chapter 7
The Last Teacher

Bill is fuming over not getting that sale. "Plus, I paid over sixty bucks on lunch with that guy." He couldn't swallow it. As he drove home, everything irritated him — the lady at the light putting on lipstick, the slow driving old-timer who made the swooping right turn, the kids walking home from school that looked so stupid with their green hair and awful clothes. *What's wrong with this world?* he thought.

Arriving home, Bill throws open the door with an ugly bang and yells, "We're *not* going to Disney World!"

"Why not?" his wife asks coming into the room.

"I didn't get the hospital sale."

"Well, that's okay, honey, we can use some of my savings this time and just do it a bit more cheaply. We can rent a little condo that has a kitchen and that will cut our expenses to less than half the cost of the resort. It'll be fun."

"How do you know how much a condo will cost?"

"I checked it all out online. There are lots of

41

really nice places to rent, and most of them have pools, as well!"

"So, you didn't even think I would get that sale, did you? Trisha, I really don't think you believe in me one bit."

"No, that's not it at all. I think the *real* problem is that you don't believe enough in yourself. Your value is not about whether or not you make a sale. Your value comes from who you are and the good you do for others. And as for me, I'm just trying to help the family have a nice summer, no matter what our finances might be right now."

Now Bill is really getting mad. "Don't preach to me with all that personal growth stuff. I'm out there battling in the real world trying to win our share. You and your friends and their airy-fairy books don't have a clue!"

"Well, one clue is that what you're doing is making both you and this whole family miserable with all your negativity."

It's a month later, and on Bill's desk are three pieces of mail; a Disney World postcard from his daughter, and a letter from his wife telling him why she's done with being around such a negative and unhappy person. And in her closing paragraph she says how much she's enjoying her new job at, of all places, Disney World!

The last piece of mail is unopened. It's an envelope from an attorney. He knows it's the divorce papers. As Bill continues sitting in his office, he begins to realize that he is not alone. He is sitting there with the *Last Teacher*, PAIN!

And that's how it works. There isn't one of us that doesn't know it. With pain it's a moment-to-moment proposition. We're all looking to avoid it at every turn, every day. And those who do it the best are the happiest, aren't they?

So, the best and wisest way to avoid pain in relationship, and in all of life, is to embrace and learn from what life is asking of us *before* it gets to the *Last Teacher*. But to do that takes a willingness to receive life's lessons with an open and trusting heart and mind. As long as we come from a place of fear and resistance, we will not be able to receive the growth and learning that life continuously offers. The more we resist what life is bringing to us, the closer the *Last Teacher* gets to our door!

This system, which includes pain as the *Last Teacher*, has been put in place in life to assist us, not to hurt us or to destroy us. We need to learn to trust the system, and the One who has put it all together.

But, how can you trust what you don't know? Ah! That's the key point! And it's from this point that life today is asking all of us to go forward. Forward to discovering firsthand Who's running the cosmic show. To do that, we have to look deep within ourselves. And when we do that, we will discover not only our Loving Source, but an all fulfilling joy and wisdom that surpasses our greatest expectations.

First you have to understand that you can't really escape from what you're here to learn. You can only postpone it. If you continue to resist life's lessons, you do so at your own peril, because if you run from them, they will chase you down and bite you in the behind. And for most of us that's a pretty tender area of our anatomy! So, once again, it's your inner wisdom and courage alone that can save the day and help you avoid another visit from the *Last Teacher*: PAIN!

Chapter 8
You Can't Trust What You Don't Know

Kevin is out on an early morning adventure. He is overflowing with joy from soaking in the glorious views of nature as he hikes along the edge of a sheer cliff that looks out toward the sun that is just beginning to boil up out of the ocean in the east. It's a stunning, beautiful sunrise.

But his joy vanishes in an instant when he catches the toe of his boot on a rock and tumbles over the edge of the cliff. He lets out a terrified scream as he plummets down the cliff face. Desperately grabbing an exposed root jutting out of the cliff face, he holds on for dear life. It's a tenuous reprieve at best, for the skinny little root seems to be pulling out of the earth as he dangles there, his life hanging from this thread.

He begins to yell. "Help, Help!! Is anybody down there?" Only silence answers back. He yells again. "God help me! Help me!"

Then a voice like the sound of the rumbling sea replies, "Let go, my son, and I will catch you."

Now Bill is silent. After a few seconds, he cries out, "Is anybody else down there?!"

And so, there it is. *"You can't trust what*

45

you don't know." This piece is a key element you must have in order to evolve to higher states of awareness, and is the core prerequisite for higher relationships. From my perspective, it is the most important thing that you will ever do.

In this story we see how critical it is to trust our Divine Source. But, we're all just like Kevin. We can't trust what we don't know. This is obviously true in the case of someone you are choosing to be in relationship with, too. But, more fundamentally, it's about first learning to trust yourself and your Source.

"Know thyself" goes the old maxim. What that's really trying to say is that you need to know your Self, the soul; as an eternal, ever-conscious ray of the Infinite Light, Love, Joy, and Intelligence that is Spirit. This is the true and authentic *you*. The ego image that you see in the bathroom mirror each morning is *not* the real you. Thank God, right?

As you become more and more in touch with your higher Self, you begin to realize, as Christ said, "I and my Father are One." Now, I'm not suggesting that you and I will attain *that* exalted state of consciousness in the near term, but that is indeed where we are all heading. And that is affirmed to us again and again by all the great ones of all the great religions.

46

But…how do you do that? What can you consciously and willfully do to lift yourself up from the lower, ego focused realms into higher states of awareness, and in doing so, accelerate your soul's evolution and thereby access the higher levels of relationship that we're focusing on? It can be said in just one word. Meditation.

"Be still and know that I Am God." "The kingdom of Heaven is within you." The fastest and most powerful way to upgrade your consciousness and dispel the delusion that you are only this mortal bag of bones is to meditate. Let's look at this more deeply from outside the context of any religion, doctrine, or dogma for a moment.

Albert Einstein wisely said: *"Problems cannot be solved at the same level of consciousness that created them."* What a great and valuable insight that is! It immediately focuses our attention in the direction we need to go in order to solve the problems at hand, whatever they may be.

What are the actual mechanics of changing our level of consciousness? I believe the best place for us to start is with the breath. Does that surprise you? Let's look at that.

It is a physiological fact that when you're

angry, the heart races and your brain becomes overheated. If this anger is not abated, it can cause physical damage to both your mental and physical well-being, and in extreme cases people have even died from excessive anger.

Unfortunately, as you well know, it is not uncommon to hear of someone becoming so angry that they attack and even kill another person. Had they been in their right mind — that is, in their normal state of consciousness — they would never have contemplated such a dark and violent act.

Now, let's see how the breath ties into these various states of consciousness. What is your breath like when you are angry? That's right; it's very rapid and shallow, and that brings about a nervous and agitated state of consciousness, doesn't it?

Now, remember how you felt when you were at a sporting event and your favorite team was struggling to win that close game. You weren't calm then, either, were you? Your heart was probably pounding as adrenaline was being pumped into your muscles, making you feel nervous with all the excitement.

Now, what if, just at that moment, someone handed you your chemistry or philosophy exam? Would you be in the optimum state of consciousness to do your best? Not a chance! You would have to calm yourself down first and get into a quiet environment in order to begin to collect your thoughts. Only then could you successfully communicate your knowledge of your subject.

There is also a direct relationship between our breath rate and our longevity. The giant tortoise, for example, breathes four times a minute and can live in excess of 300 years! Whereas, the restless monkey breathes about 32 times a minute and has an average life span of about 25 years, which is less than 10% of our slow moving and slow breathing friend, the tortoise. This is worth thinking about in relation to our own longevity, where we see that people who are relatively calmer than their nervous counterparts often live much healthier, happier, and longer lives.

So, thinking about the calmer and slower end of the breath spectrum, have you ever noticed when you're really concentrating on something you aren't paying attention to anything else around you, and sometimes you may not even hear someone speak to you, or hear the phone ring? What is your breath like when you are concentrating like that? Have you noticed?

It's very slow and calm, isn't it? In fact, the calmer and more concentrated the mind is, the quieter and slower the breath.

Now we can relate the breath back to what Albert Einstein said. *"Problems cannot be solved at the same level of consciousness that created them."* With this understanding, we now see that when the breath is calm the mind can concentrate much more powerfully. It is here, then, that we begin to realize that we actually *do* have a powerful tool that can help us change the level of our consciousness whenever we feel the need.

The science of this process, the calming and controlling of the breath and the mind, comes to us from the culture of ancient India, where it has been in practice for more than 5,000 years. This science of concentration and breath control is known the world over as meditation. And I wholeheartedly recommend it to you as the greatest and most powerful tool for accelerating your soul's evolution that can be found in our world today!

The reason that meditation is so effective in up-leveling our consciousness is that it helps us still the mind sufficiently enough so that we can see more clearly into the calm, crystal clear *mirror* of our souls!

Chapter 9
In The Mirror

From Lewis Carroll's children's classic, *Through The Looking Glass*, we get an ideal metaphor that reflects the journey that is calling to each of us. For all of life's *real work and adventure takes place in and through the mirror. That is, in and through the mirror of introspection.

Earlier we looked at the empowerment that comes from dropping the delusive drug of "victim consciousness," and we also discovered a valuable tool to help us counteract negative thoughts and feelings. And so, we begin to see from those first two pieces that everyone who strives for self-transformation must work from the inside out, because our real work in life is always *"in the mirror."*

We are all in this world to change ourselves, not others. Yet, when we do change ourselves, others are helped because we are all connected. It always starts from the inside out. It begins from within each individual who awakens to the truth that it is "I" who needs to improve. That's why I love the metaphor *in the mirror*.

---

* Soul evolving work

It is spiritual ignorance and immaturity to blame conditions on others. It is not truth, and it is this type of thinking that perpetuates darkness in the consciousness of mankind. The real work is always about changing ourselves.

So, if you're presently in an unhealthy or toxic relationship the only way it will change is if one or both people make changes in their consciousness. Otherwise, nothing improves. New jobs, new cars, new hairdos, and new romances are all great, but those things have nothing to do with you experiencing a healthier relationship that will exhibit more intimacy, fuller acceptance, greater love, nurturing, and appreciation.

In order to receive those gifts from another person, you first have to know that you truly deserve them, and then also be willing to fully offer those very same gifts to your partner. This is because, in the highest expressions of relationship, partners are equal, free, and share unconditional love and support for each other.

So if *you* desire to be loved, honored, nurtured, respected, appreciated and enjoyed as an equal partner, then you must first realize that you also deserve those things, and that you have that very same intention in offering those unconditional gifts from your heart to your partner.

Before we talk more about the giving, I'd like to talk with you about the other half of the coin, *"the getting."* Have you ever been told that "you're no good" (and that can take a thousand forms) by a parent, a sibling, a teacher, a spouse or even a stranger? I think most of us have in some form or another.

Well, these experiences create both psychic and emotional damage because they can take away a portion of our belief in ourselves. And we all know of extreme cases where people no longer have much self-regard. It doesn't have to be all that obvious to be damaging and debilitating. The point is that, bit-by-bit, our self-esteem can be eroded away.

Of course, life is a two-way street. You can also have self-esteem building experiences, as well. But for most of us it's a mixed bag, and it means that it may not be easy to believe that we can have a relationship that will bring us all that I just described. In part that is because most people can't imagine a life too far afield from what they're presently experiencing. Sure, there are the reveries where we imagine "the perfect life and partner," but is there a core belief in truly deserving it and being able to have it?

Remember, all of creation is a huge test. It is, in fact, a cosmic game where you and I are challenged to discover and recover our awareness of our true Self, our all powerful and glorious soul-Self. And in playing out our various roles across the ever-changing backdrop of the ages, we gradually learn life's lessons and begin to build stronger and better character traits to help us on our way. It often seems like a slow and painful journey. Perhaps you've noticed!

Think about this, too. Why do we get a brand new day to live and act in, every day? It's so ridiculously obvious! We always get a new day in order for us to have a chance to start over and do it better than we did it yesterday. Perfection is beyond the top of the mountain. I don't think we ever truly get there in this world. But, we can see and feel which direction it is and follow our heart's calling to guide us on our way.

One of the best ways to help yourself stay physically and emotionally healthy as you travel your road each new day is to love and forgive *yourself* enough to start over in a clean and optimistic way — every single day. Starting over as the person who is a little more caring and loving than you were yesterday, and starting over by being someone who is wise enough to not take the emotional baggage of yesterday's hurts, errors, and losses with you into all your new tomorrows.

In addition, there's even more good news hot off the cosmic calendar. This is the beginning of a new and uplifting age, one that is now offering us accelerated course work where we can speed up our journey, not only to healthier relationships, but also to a greater expansion of consciousness, of which more rewarding relationships are just one of the wonderful results.

The best way to take advantage of this evolutionary opportunity is by taking a "Spiritual Bath" every day. Learning to still the noisy mind allows you to calm your emotions in order to access your higher faculties of intuition. This will help you gain fresh insights and a more enlightened understanding about the various challenges that come to you at any given time.

Another great benefit of the daily habit of quieting the ever-busy mind and its colluding partner, the ego, is that you can quickly and easily cleanse away the hurts, the disappointments, the dullness, and meanness we often encounter in our daily contact with the world. This is what I call divine refreshment. And who doesn't need some of that every day?

The whole purpose of life is to evolve our

consciousness higher and higher until, at last, we are reunited with our Cosmic Parent. This requires us to increase and purify both our wisdom and our love so that we can conquer ever-vaster territories of darkness by replacing their governance with the glorious light and love of our souls. And it is meditation that makes one an ever-increasingly powerful carrier of the light.

When the tail wags the dog, when the ego shouts down the soul, you lose your way and all the pettiness of the ego's world then dominates your consciousness with littleness and pain. So, it's time to stop *worshiping the lesser gods* of greed, selfishness, gossip, lying, exclusiveness, sense attachments, meanness and grudges; all those limiting qualities that block the magnetism of higher relationships and higher consciousness.

It is The Cup of Your Heart that needs the most repair, because when it's empty or broken, you have nothing to pour out unto others. When it is kept full by daily replenishment from the Infinite Source within, then you not only have love and healing for yourself, but you will have an unending supply of love, joy, and healing energy to pour out unto others. It is right here, then, that you can see the tremendous importance of *your role* in being part of the solution of love, rather than part of the problem of ignorance and pain.

So, I implore you to keep polishing your internal mirror so that you can reflect to the world and to your *intimate other* the beauty of what you're really all about!

Chapter 10
The Knight

With body, pride, and honor all wounded, still he rides on through the darkness. The rain driven sideways by the screaming wind is a relentless frontal assault. A thousand liquid spears add to the agony of each breath's pull against the phantom rib that long ago had been ripped out of him. It was a bad night to be a knight.

In the hopeful first rays of morning, Adam, a name heavy with the significance of his quest, looks out upon a-dam that has long held back all that he has ever been afraid to feel, lest it carry him to ruin.

He knows she's there, waiting for him behind the wall. He knows further that to retrieve his sword from "The Lady of the Man-made Lake" he will have to strike an equal alliance with her. The cold fear of it makes the previous night's suffering appear as but a trifle.

Yet he knows it is the Great God Herself who keeps pushing him forward up the steep and rocky mountain of his prejudices. Against his own ego's will, he watches in disbelief as each foot somehow falls into a natural rhythm that just now brings him to the very edge of his living lake of dread.

There she is, shimmering, ghost like, just below the surface. He recognizes the face of Eve seen in a hundred thousand subconscious mirrors. Dropping to his knees, his rough hands gripped in wordless pleading, he at last groans out the primal truth. *"I need you!"*

The Truth Revealed Frees All. The sword pierces up from the lake. He lunges forward and grasps it to his breast, and in that instant The Lady of the Lake enters into him and he is whole again, at last.

As souls, we are neither man nor woman. But here in creation we're required to wear the garb of male and female, as you may have noticed! And with that comes a whole host of challenges, doesn't it?

Beyond the obvious physiological differences between the sexes are the mental, emotional, and psychological differences. And for our discussion today, we can distill these down to one concept. Man has *reason* dominant in his nature, and woman has *feeling* dominant.

In no way do I mean to imply that woman doesn't reason and man doesn't feel. We all know reasoning women and feeling men. But, like in my story, in order for us to have an inner sense of completeness, we must learn to embrace and integrate both qualities, reason and feeling.

Just like in a successful marriage where each person is loved, honored, respected, nurtured, and appreciated as an equal, there also needs to be a successful relationship within ourselves that honors both reason and feeling as equal partners in guiding the ship of our lives on its journey through this challenging world.

And please understand. This is an internal integration. This is not suggesting that men need to be more feminine or that women should be more masculine. Rather, this is about coming to the realization that life is asking each of us to more fully develop and integrate both our reasoning faculties and our feeling nature by blending them into a balanced expression of who we *really* are as wise and loving souls. But even greater than this is the unexpected bonus that comes with the accomplishment of this great integration.

A parallel example taken from the physical world is like when you blend the right amounts of oxygen and hydrogen. You get a completely different and wonderful thing. You get water! Likewise, when we can fully integrate both the rational and the feeling sides of our nature into a balance, we rise up to the next level in our spiritual evolution. We find that we have awakened the higher quality of *intuition* and its power of direct perception of Truth.

And as ideal exemplars that model both the value and beauty of this illuminating integration, I would offer you the names of Jesus, Krishna, and Gautama the Buddha!

Chapter 11
Environment

It has been said that environment is stronger than willpower. That's both scary and revealing. We'd all like to think that with our willpower we could always direct ourselves to make the right choices and take the appropriate actions in any environment. But every year we see that everyone from priests to presidents falter and don't. Yet, I do think there eventually comes a time when we do have that level of self-control, discrimination, and wisdom so that we can. Most of us, however, don't start out with that fully in place. Perhaps that's why the Creative Intelligence created parents, teachers, mentors, and good friends.

As a young boy, I had two close friends. One was close by geography and the other was close by the quality of his character and true friendship. One lived at the end of my block, while the other lived a couple of miles away. The boy on the corner was a year older than me and physically stronger, as well. He always had lots of ideas on how to spend our time. A lot of those ideas were definitely not good. Throwing rocks at cats, siphoning gas out of cars parked across the street from the nearby bowling alley, stealing money from unsuspecting donors to his paper drives, and more. Well, I had enough discrimination to avoid most of his out-of-control behaviors, but not all. Having him in my life on a nearly daily basis got me into some bad habits and bad ways of thinking.

The other boy, Peder, lived near the junior and senior high schools that we attended. Pete was an only surviving child, his older brother having died at the age of seven. His father was a music professor at the local college and his mom was a homemaker. Homemaker, now there's a job classification that is way underrated! I can remember going to his home for lunch on many a school day where hot bowls of soup with sandwiches, cut corner-to-corner, awaited our noontime arrival.

There in that sunny kitchen nook we ate our nutritious lunch under the loving eyes of his mother. Peder couldn't play after school like most of the boys. He had to go home and sit at his desk in his bedroom and do his homework; again, under the watchful eyes of his mother.

My mom worked full-time downtown for an insurance company, getting up at 5:00 a.m. and making lunches for all six of us before she blew out the door on her way to catch the 7:00 bus to work. Dad had three part-time jobs and took a full-time load of courses at Fresno State during those years, working toward his accounting degree. In this setting there was plenty of time for me to avoid homework and get into trouble. A young tree, without being tethered to a guiding stake, usually will not grow straight and strong.

My grades in high school got worse with each passing year. The more homework a class required, the lower the grade I'd get on my report card. My folks said all the right things, but they did not walk their talk. They did not sit down with their son and get him into the appropriate habit patterns.

Now, ultimately, we are each responsible for our own actions and choices, but good parenting is obviously highly important for every child. The good news is that life gave me additional opportunities to clean up some of those poor habits. So, by the time I returned from the Vietnam War and went back to finish my B.A., I was then mature enough to discipline myself to do what needed to be done. But not everyone can turn things around as easily as I did back then. Why not?

The deeper truth is that we are not building on the experiences of just one lifetime. And, as unpleasant as this may be to acknowledge for some, it is we, as souls, who pick our parents. And that choosing is not a hit or miss process. Just like in relationship, it is a matching of vibrations, and not necessarily in the ways we might first imagine. It matches in ways that create a new set of conditions that will deliver to us what we need to learn next.

Now, factor in what we can call good and bad karma. And by the way, I really don't think the "good" and "bad" terminology is the right way to look at it. In the ultimate sense it is the Intelligent Universe that is always responding to whatever choices we make in order to help us move forward, even when those responses bring us pain.

The point is that this is a cause and effect universe, and this law applies to every step of the way on our soul's journey to enlightenment. When we see something that seems blatantly unfair and tragic in the human context that we just cannot accept, it can be understood in a soul context. For in the ultimate sense, we are all here in this world to profit our souls, not our egos.

The important thing for our discussion is to realize that once we understand the importance of environment, we need to pay close attention to it, because everything is vibration. And all vibrations are either supportive of your efforts to elevate your consciousness, or they are trying to pull your consciousness down. What we concentrate upon is what we add to our consciousness. This is why both the internal and external environments of 12-step programs like *Alcoholics Anonymous* are valuable aids in recovering from addictions.

Music is another great example of environments. Some music can lift you up and other music can pull you down. Reading inspirational books is uplifting. I like to read biographies that show how people have overcome their personal challenges, and then gone on to meaningful successes in their lives. In contrast, reading trashy novels will pull you down.

TV, also, has its obvious high and low expressions, and it's something that can pull you down if you let your consciousness soak in its negative and lower expressions. The people you live with, work with, play with, and study with are all part of your environment, as well.

The thoughts that you choose to let dominate your mind and feelings are one of the most influential environments of all. And it is *this* environment that you have complete control over. You just have to pay attention to it. If you don't, bad habits can set in and run your life into the ditch of unhappiness.

It is also helpful to not dig up and over-analyze problems with unproductive, negative mental probing. Rather, it is better to focus your thoughts on the positive by concentrating on what will bring you lasting happiness and feelings of self-accomplishment. You should make the mental effort to build the habit of consistently putting your energy and concentration on those things that nurture your highest hopes and aspirations.

This will help you pull out the weeds of doubt and moods from your consciousness by adding the sunshine of positive thinking and acting that you empower and replenish each day through regular meditation. This is how you can fuel the vehicle of your consciousness to take you across the abyss of life's pain and sorrow, and deliver you to the vaster fields of wisdom, joy, and fulfillment.

Consequently, both your mental and physical environments can be either your best friends or your worst enemies, because your mind operates like an amazing magnetic sponge, soaking up whatever you focus it on. Therefore, are you going to choose to regularly dip the sponge of your mind in the pure lake of beauty and inspiration, or will you ignorantly make a habit of soaking up that which is unwholesome and toxic?

So, be careful about what you choose to do, because the habit-forming mechanism of your mind can either help you or hurt you. Bottom line, to successfully guard, nurture, and uplift your body, mind and soul, you need to consistently pay attention to both your inner and your outer environments. Both your physical and mental environments are vital elements in helping you accelerate your evolution and increase your happiness, and therefore are essential ingredients in preparing you for a higher and more fulfilling relationship.

Chapter 12
Willpower vs. Addiction

When we are under the influence of an addiction, we find that there is little or no energy to resist whatever is keeping us from using our willpower to overcome what has gotten a negative hold on our consciousness. Whether it's an addiction to drugs, rage, alcohol, sex, overeating, wrong eating, or negative patterns of thinking, fighting it from the same level of consciousness that created the addiction doesn't really work.

That's because it is putting your already habituated ego-driven mind in charge of your recovery program, which is like putting a fox in charge of your security program at your chicken ranch. It is definitely not going to work!

Here's why. It doesn't work because the *opposite* of willpower *is* addiction! Therefore, when you are under the spell of an addiction, there is automatically little or no willpower to help you fight your way to freedom from the addiction. But Einstein's golden key, *"You cannot solve a problem at the same level of consciousness that created it..."* gets us going in the right direction.

I am not a substance abuse counselor, psychologist, or psychiatrist. Those professionals dedicate themselves to the healing arts using their tools and their modalities, and they have my respect. But it is time these health care professionals discover the missing piece in recovery programs today. Energy!

From my window, I'd like to offer you a view that perhaps you'll see like a hologram, looking into the problem from another angle that gives you a more holistic and three-dimensional vantage point by incorporating the spiritual and energetic perspectives — and in doing so, underscore Einstein's principle that we need to solve problems from a level that is higher than where they were created.

From those who have achieved elevated states of consciousness, we know that the higher the consciousness goes, the more powerful it becomes. Hence, the increase of *willpower* is a natural result of raising your consciousness! So, for those of you who yearn for freedom from an addiction, this is the ladder that will get you out of that dark hole...if you will make the effort to climb!

For those who don't make the effort to use their free will to raise their consciousness, and instead allow their consciousness to continue to go down, down to more abuse of their bodies, their minds, or others, they will automatically find that they are giving up increasing amounts of their willpower. And if that's not bad enough, the lower the consciousness goes, the less discrimination you have, and so the potential to spiral down and down, even to an animalistic state, is real and observable in every society.

Let's make sure we have the full understanding that addiction is not limited to just drugs. Addictions are anything that you can't control and use your free will to move away from, like moods, gossiping, anger, eating issues, smoking, victim consciousness, and the addictive habit of fear that is based in lack of trust in the Divine Benevolence.

Addiction is anything that you relinquish your power to, which thereby lowers your level of consciousness that then makes you an energetic match for lower relationships and lower expressions of life experiences, and the resultant pain that comes from ignorant choices and behaviors.

So remember, wisdom is power...if you act upon it! If you realize that addictions destroy your willpower, and with it your power to be unconditionally happy, healthy, and successful, you'll pay attention to those things that, inch by inch, can steal away your power to control your own destiny.

Let's now go deeper into this topic with a visual description. Behind our physical body of fleshly matter is an extremely powerful, fully conscious and intelligent matrix of light and energy that produces and sustains our physicality. This is your energy body with its main dynamo located at the top of the spine in the brain region. And from there, intelligent life-energy flows down into the six plexuses of the spine that act as sub-dynamos, where they send out their intelligent, life-sustaining light and energy to the various regions of the body that each one serves.

With that picture in place, you can see what can happen if there is abuse of the physical body. In doing so, you are damaging the body vehicle that you need to work with in raising your consciousness and accelerating your evolution by not being able to receive the intelligent healing light and energy that is trying to flow into your body and your life. This, of course, is especially bad if you are damaging your brain cells, either through substance abuse or some other form of mental or emotional abuse.

Further, when you are under the influence of addictions, the life force in your energy body can become dominantly locked up in the lower centers of consciousness in your spine. Consequently, you get to where you are no longer able to have the higher perceptions and understanding of life that express all of the more evolved character qualities that make life more enjoyable and worthwhile, and help you take your evolution forward. Bottom line, addictions are among your worst enemies, because they can steal every one of your spiritual and material treasures.

Fortunately, that's not the end of the story. There is some really good news, too. Actually, it's great news! There is a powerful and simple way to reverse these energetic tendencies. The Divine Intelligence has provided for every contingency. In doing so, it has given us perfect tools to help us reverse these negative patterns by redirecting our life energy in a positive and uplifting direction. So that we can actually pull our attention away from those destructive habits and patterns that are not serving us, and refocus it on serving our higher aspirations.

These tools are collectively known to the spiritually wise as meditation. And through the power of meditation you can gain the ability to consciously redirect your energy away from your old, misery-making, addictive thoughts and actions and put yourself in touch with your Source and your higher Self. In so doing, you give yourself back the power to rebuild your willpower, your ability to create new and healthier patterns of thinking and living,[*] and thus, empower yourself to create a new and more rewarding vision of who you really are.

---

[*] *Your Maximum Mind* (New York: Random House, 1987) By Herbert Benson, M. D., Professor of Medicine, Harvard Medical School "Through meditation... you can set the stage for important mind- and habit-altering brain change."

"It's largely the established circuits of the left side of the brain that are telling us, 'You can't change your way of living...Your bad habits are forever... You're just made in a certain way, and you have to live with that fact.' That simply is not true."

"Scientific research has shown that electrical activity between the left and right sides of the brain becomes coordinated during certain kinds of meditation and prayer." Through these processes, the mind definitely becomes more capable of being altered and having its capacities maximized.... When you are in this state of enhanced left-right hemispheric communication ... 'plasticity of cognition' occurs, in which you actually change the way you view the world.... If you focus or concentrate on some form of written passage which represents the direction in which you wish you life to be heading, [this] more directed thought process will help you to rewire the circuits in your brain in more positive directions.... When we change our patterns of thinking and acting, the brain cells begin to establish additional connections, or 'new wirings.' These new connections then communicate in fresh ways with other cells, and before long, the pathways or wirings that kept the phobia or other habit alive are replaced or altered.... Changed actions and a changed life will follow."

The spiritually wise know and live life from this understanding: The *game of life* is an energy ballgame!

The following story illustrates wonderfully this powerful truth. In one of the old *Star Wars* movies, the Clone Army of thousands of clones is routing the good guys. It is absolutely ballgame over, when all of a sudden every single one of the clones falls down dead! What the heck happened?

Somebody pulled the plug at the main dynamo! And in so doing, the source of their energy was cut off. Miraculously, in the eleventh hour, the day was saved!

This is what meditation can do for you. It can save the day, and your life, no matter how far down you may have slipped. It does so by cutting off the energy to whatever old habits and patterns you've been trying to get rid of, and helps you redirect that energy to the positive purposes you desire to accomplish in your life.

And that's only the beginning. Through meditation you can discover the unlimited potential of your soul. Meditation is, indeed, the ultimate tool of liberation that has been cherished and extolled by saints from both east and west from time immemorial.

Learning to meditate is like going back to the Cosmic Manufacturer in order to download new and better software to run your life. You'll then be empowered to run new and better programs and patterns in your consciousness, and through the wisdom supported actions that follow, be able to replace all the old "corrupted software" that has run your life into the ditch of suffering and stolen both your willpower and your dignity.

This, then, is how all negative and addictive behaviors can be overcome and replaced with powerful, new, healthy patterns. The psychological models of the last century have been very limited in their effectiveness to solve these life-threatening challenges, because they lack the understanding of the most important factor of all: Energy. For where the mind is, there will the heart be also! And there is no greater tool for developing mind and body control than meditation. It is the science for the new age. I believe this science of learning to interiorize and master the mind will take us a long way forward in upgrading and replacing the old, limited, drug-based medical and psychological models in the healing arts.

Through the use of the "energy and meditation" model, the consciousness is gradually lifted to increasingly higher states of awareness by the refocusing of our attention and concentration upon the new healthy patterns we want to create in our lives.   In so doing, the old, negative patterns and addictions are "starved out" because there is no longer any energy there to sustain them.

There is, of course, a Spiritual component in all of this, as I mentioned. For the more we up-level our consciousness, the more in tune we become with our Loving Source; hence, the more power and support we receive from this attunement to win these great battles of life!

I know it's completely obvious to you now that in working to overcome addictions through the control and redirection of your life energy, you will be on your way to higher consciousness, higher character qualities, and the *higher relationships* that magnetically match who you *really* are.

All of this is a long and holy journey for every one of us. As long as you are here in this world, that obviously means you still have some work to do — evolutionary, soul enlightening work to do. But, the wonderful point is that if you continually work at up-leveling your consciousness, you will be putting yourself more and more in alignment to manifest the more joyous and fulfilling relationship you are seeking. This is how the laws of the universe work. When you realize that you can consciously put them to work in your life, then you are acting from soul guidance, not binding ego patterns. And the results are both abundant and joyous!*

Much of what you quest after in life can be accomplished by first *becoming* what you seek. If you want the relationship you're seeking to be a constant source of joy and inspiration to you because of the unconditional love, intimacy, wisdom, and happiness it showers on you every single day, then you need to refine your consciousness so that you can fully offer those same gifts to your *intimate other,* and in so doing create your half of this *perfect match.* The intelligent, magnetic power of Spirit that is resident in you *will* create a match that is a perfect fit with whatever level of consciousness, high or low, you are at.

So, if addictions are blocking your way forward, you can use the science of meditation to pull the plug from the energy grid of attention that is feeding the addiction, and then redirect

---

* "The harvest is plenteous, but the laborers are few." Matthew 9:37

your mind, and the energy it guides, to help you build the new habits and new patterns that will support your healthy intentions and permanently defeat the enemy by taking away the energy that has been powering it.

Chapter 13
The New Relationship Killing Drug: *Internet Pornography*

The Problem

Recent statistics state:[*]

• More than 70% of men from 18 to 34 visit a pornographic site monthly.

• Breakdown of men / women visitors to pornography sites: 72% men - 28% women.

• 9.4 million women access adult websites each month.

• Revenue from US pornography exceeds the combined revenues of the four major TV networks and is bigger than the *combined* revenues of all professional football, basketball and baseball franchises.

• Worldwide, the pornography industry is larger than the *combined* revenues of all the top technology companies: Microsoft, Google, Amazon, eBay, Yahoo, Apple, Netflix and EarthLink and estimated to be over 100 billion dollars annually.

• Nine out of 10 children ages 8-16 have

---

[*] Statistics Source: *Covenant Eyes* "The Standard for Internet Integrity"

been exposed to pornography on the Internet.

- 10% of adults *admit* to Internet sexual addiction.
- 1/3 of all visitors to all adult web sites are women.
- 20% of men *admit* accessing pornography at work.
- A recent poll showed 47% percent of families said pornography is a problem in their home.
- *Today's Christian Woman Magazine* reported: 34% of female readers of their online newsletter admitted to intentionally accessing Internet porn.
- One popular pro-adultery site shows 92% of male members and 60% of female members are married. A new member joins this one site every 15 seconds.

The American Academy of Matrimonial Lawyers reported that the two most salient factors in divorce cases today are:

- 68% of all divorces involved one party meeting a new lover over the Internet.
- 56% involved one party having "an obsessive interest in pornographic websites."

The Effects*:*

In my original outline for this book, I had no thought of giving this subject special attention. But a wise and caring young man pleaded with me to include the pornography issue, because he recognized it as a huge problem in his generation that was dramatically impacting tens and perhaps hundreds of thousands of relationships in a very negative way. Well, it didn't take much research to figure out that he was completely right. The statistics make the problem undeniable.

This subject could be a whole book in itself, but that's not my intent here. I want to add this piece in order to give you an esoteric way of gaining freedom from this rampant problem as part of the process of refining and up-leveling your consciousness, especially as it applies to relationship. So let's take it from there.

The great American sage of the nineteenth century, Ralph Waldo Emerson, said, *"Man descends to meet."* What did he actually mean by that? I interpret his statement to mean that when we are exclusively in outer consciousness, we are also in a lower state of consciousness.

But when our consciousness is interiorized, our attention is in our heart and brain areas, where the higher centers of awareness and intuition reign. And from that state we can think, feel, and act in a higher, more evolved and enlightened way.

When we live our lives exclusively in the outer consciousness of the body, thinking that that is all we are, then we're functioning only from a sense of our egos and the senses, and therefore are oblivious to our real soul nature. Remember, in this world we are engaged in a tremendous battle of light vs. dark, ego vs. soul; and that the negative forces are always trying to pull us down. That's their job! And as you can see, the Dark Side is being hugely successful with pornography. So much so that this problem is rapidly becoming the new mental health challenge of our world today. Why?

Second in power only to the instinct for survival is the sexual desire to procreate. The sex impulse is natural and powerful in every human being. But when it is overemphasized and used like a drug to temporarily anesthetize our feelings with a temporary high, the results are very damaging. It not only compromises our long-term health and vitality, but even more significantly, it can lower our consciousness more and more into an animalistic state.

Energetically, the sexual instinct is centered at the base of the spine, which corresponds with the lowest center of consciousness. What happens is the lower we allow our consciousness to sink and dwell in that lower state, the further we take ourselves from the ability to be unconditionally happy because our journey to enlightenment and unconditional happiness lies in the opposite direction.

Therefore, it is a journey of learning how to lift our consciousness into higher and higher states in order to discover our true nature. And that, as I've pointed out, has a lot to do with energy. The result is that the more we can redirect this sexual energy to be used in higher pursuits, the more we evolve, and the more unconditional happiness we will access.

Some good examples here are the many saints and sages whose lives have long shined as idyllic models for mankind. Why are they the very happiest among us? One of the reasons is that they understand the value in making the effort to redirect their powerful sexual energy into more creative, useful, and evolving expressions.

One of the most important things we must remember is that we are not just biological beings. We are souls that have a body. And our soul needs to be in charge. When it's not, this type of addiction is the kind of disaster that can take over our lives.

So, by ignorantly choosing *lust over love,* we spiral down and down, farther and farther into the land of ever-increasing depression and addiction by desperately seeking to anesthetize ourselves with the endorphins that are released with an orgasm.

This momentary high becomes more and more difficult to achieve and sustain because it is a bogus strategy that can never bring us any lasting happiness. And the reason for that, once again, is that we are *not* the body! We are, in fact, the soul. That's why the answer lies in the opposite direction. We have to learn to lift the energy from the sexual regions to the heart and brain regions where we can more easily make choices that benefit our higher intentions, and thereby bring us a much higher level of happiness and contentment.

Remember that when addictions begin to take hold of our consciousness, our willpower becomes increasingly weakened because willpower and addiction are at opposite ends of the scale of self-determination. And without understanding the need to redirect the energy in the body, the outlook is not very good because of the increasing loss of our willpower.

But by learning to redirect the *energy* from the sexual regions to the heart and brain regions, recovery can definitely be accomplished. This is the tremendous power that meditation can give you in your quest for freedom from addiction!

Now, let's look a bit more at the physiological side of the problem. This story will give you some quick insights. Not long ago, I watched a PBS nature program that focused on the mating habits of a large and beautiful variety of African antelope. The males of this species compete to collect large groups of females. Then, during mating season, the largest and strongest males mate several times a day for nearly two months. The result is that, toward the end of the mating season, many of these large male animals were completely exhausted; some even had difficulty just standing up. This made them extremely easy prey for lions.

It is even worse for humans, because the human physiology is not made for repeated sexual encounters over short periods of time. Those who study and practice the higher levels of yoga understand that control of the sexual life-energy in the body is a fundamental factor in health, longevity, and in mental and emotional wellbeing, as well. So, by the loss of this vital life-energy through excessive sexual indulgence, the health and vitality of the nervous system, as well as the overall immune system, are increasingly compromised.

The *emotional effects* of this addiction are even more damaging, especially for women. For those women who are in a relationship where the man is addicted to pornography, they will typically and naturally feel degraded and threatened by his actions because the purpose and result of pornography is to view and use women only to stimulate and fulfill man's lowest expressions of lust. This is an extremely powerful tool of the Dark Side in our current age, and its successes are destroying relationships everywhere.

This kind of addictive behavior can quickly destroy a woman's sense of equality, personal value, and safety in the relationship. Most women in relationship are the emotional and spiritual fortress of the home and the family, where every member comes to feel safe, nurtured, valued, and loved. And when the man, husband or father becomes addicted to these lower behavior patterns, it can quickly destroy both the psychological and spiritual fabric of both the relationship and the family.

Of course, there is a flipside to this, and the same scenario can play out when the genders are reversed with the results being just as damaging and destructive for men.

The Solution:

I believe addiction is the greatest weapon of the Dark Side in creation, because it erodes willpower, health, relationships, self-esteem, and hope. When you feel hopeless, you believe there is no further value in resisting the enemy, so you give up. As long as you believe you are defeated, the enemy will continue to have power over you, keeping you locked up in the dungeon of intense suffering and delusion.

Here's how you can break free. You must first understand that the enemy *must be fought* on all levels, physically, mentally, emotionally, and spiritually. And because the enemy is an intelligent force in creation, it is extremely important that you totally commit to throwing all your resources and all your weapons into the sacred battle to recover your physical, mental, emotional, and spiritual strength, and thereby your self respect and your soul's freedom to live your life according to your highest aspirations. This is what I call "living your life on purpose."

In this colossal battle of life, every victory you gain, no matter how small, brings increased strength and support to every other area of your life. Everything is interrelated. From this you can see the value of staying vigilant in becoming stronger in every area of your life, and not avoiding any area that may be particularly challenging for you. Remember this: It doesn't matter how many times you fall down. It only matters how many times you get up! This is a key principle for winning in every area of your life.

Let's start now by reviewing the basics, beginning with the body. Regular exercise is a necessity in maintaining both physical and mental health. Everyone knows that. A weak body can also lead to a weak will and a weakening of the mind. Personally, I've found that vigorous daily exercise is a great "mood buster." And it's also a concrete way to redirect sexual energy! So, it's vital that you do everything you can to keep the body fit and free from toxins.

Saint Francis called the body "brother donkey." Why? He called it "brother donkey" because he recognized that he had a body and he had a mind, but that he *was* a soul. I encourage you to try to live your life from this spiritual principle. It will help give you additional power to control your thoughts, feelings and actions.

It is also very important to remember that the mind does not have perfect vision, either. So, the need to cultivate your spiritual nature by developing your intuition is paramount. When you learn to contact your higher self through regular meditation, the power of intuition begins to guide your life to higher and higher levels of understanding, self-control, and happiness. So, as you can see, life requires us to work on all three levels, body, mind, and soul.

Diet is an integral component in dealing with sexual addictions, as well. It is a far more significant factor than most people realize. Mahatma Gandhi counseled his followers to pursue a vegetarian diet because he knew that to gain control of and redirect the sexual energy, one needs to have control over the *palate*.

Therefore, I highly recommend that you eliminate as many toxins from your diet as possible, because it's important to understand that toxins deplete our energy and overall health, and overly spicy foods stimulate the sexual regions of the body.

Red meats, especially beef and pork, are highly toxic and are difficult for the body to assimilate. Because they drag the consciousness down, it would be of tremendous positive value for you to move away from those heavily toxic meats. If a fully vegetarian diet doesn't suit you, then I'd recommend that you limit your meat intake to chicken and fish, as I do. Your "donkey" will be really grateful, and you will be helping the shift of energy into your higher centers of consciousness just by making these simple dietary adjustments.

As I touched on earlier, a healthy mind is also an obvious prerequisite to being a happy individual. And that requires right habits of thinking. Positive thinking precedes positive acting. Like the body, the mind needs to be exercised properly every day in a conscious and positive manner. That can take lots of different forms, like practicing positive affirmations, reading good books, serving and helping others, training your mind to look for the positive and the good in everything you encounter, and cultivating an attitude that is grateful for everything that comes to you in life.

Paying close attention to your inner "self talk" can also be very empowering and revealing as to the condition of your mental environment. Becoming a more aware and positive individual comes from building your mental and emotional muscles. You have to work at it. Remember, the Dark Side is always at work trying to pull you down. So, there is no avoiding this battle of life. And when you make the mental effort to be and act in a positive and grateful manner, you'll really appreciate the positive effects it creates in your consciousness and in improving your interactions with others. Your overall mental health is an integral part of healthy and happy relationships.

It is the same with your emotions. But, with emotions we find that feelings tend to follow our thoughts. For example: *"Oh that's terrible. I feel sad."* You judged whatever it was first with your mind, and then added your appropriate emotional response.

"Where the mind is, there will the heart be, also." So, your emotions mirror back to you how you feel about your life's experiences and choices. From my experience, my emotions are like my little brother and sister. Wherever my mind goes, they follow right along. I believe that is why we can't control our emotions until we can first control our behavior. And behavioral choices start first with the mind.

Further, choosing the right environments for body, mind, and soul create for you powerful physic protection on your journey through this world. And we all need all the help we can get!

Every one of the things I've mentioned so far will definitely help you. But the *greatest and most powerful weapon* you can use is daily meditation. This is how you can do problem solving from a level higher than where the problem was created, and brings with it a powerful and more all-encompassing solution. Here's why.

By creating a daily meditation practice, the power of your inwardly focused mind automatically begins to withdraw the life force from the nervous system, especially the sex organs, and begins to centralize it in the brain cells where you are better able to stimulate the creation of new, good habits and help to starve out the old former habits of unwanted addictions.[*]

Meditation is indeed your most powerful tool in overcoming any addiction because it pulls the plug on the energy grid that is powering the addiction or unwanted habit. Understanding this energy component is truly a new dispensation to the world that will help us free ourselves from the clutches of the Dark Side and the sense of hopelessness that it has fostered throughout the Dark Ages. So, if you persevere in the practice of both wisdom and energy control, you will, in time, find your long hoped for freedom from addiction!

All right, let's review the powerful pieces you now have in your arsenal to help you defeat the army on the other side of the battlefield:

*1. **__The Powerful Desire to Change__** your life and the actions that have created this addiction.*

---

* See footnote, page 76

*2. **The Light of Wisdom**, which you've gained by thoroughly understanding the destructive effects of this addiction.*

*3. **Environment:** Choosing good environments and good friends who support your high intentions while avoiding those settings and people that try to pull you down.*

*4. **Willpower,** given to you by Spirit, to help you choose good over evil any time any place.*

*5. **The Power to Lift and Redirect Your Life Energy** from the region of the sex organs to the brain by creating a daily meditation practice.*

*6. **Divine Assistance,** which you can call on through your willingness to commit to doing whatever you need to do to defeat the enemy within and without by acknowledging that you can't do it alone. By cultivating an attitude of gratitude and willingness, you create the right mental and spiritual environment that will draw Divine Assistance.*

*7. **Understanding How to Use the Power of the Mind** By learning to focus your attention and your energy on solutions, rather than upon problems, for "Where the mind is there will the heart be, also."*

Other Useful and Common Sense Tools

1. Disabling access on your computers to adult sites. If you're on a diet, it helps to remove culprits from the cupboard.

2. Substitute positive action when attacked by the urge to engage in destructive behavior. Deep breathing is great. So is getting up from your desk, walking away physically, and going outside to breathe or exercise. Any positive action is using your will to build positive new habit patterns.

3. Turn your thoughts away from negative patterns by focusing on your goal. Have a mental or visual reminder that is easy to access and easy to see, like a picture of your wife or family.

4. And, of course, what's absolutely the best is to <u>combine them all</u>! Get up from the desk; pick up the picture while saying your affirmation, then go outside and exercise. Repeat your routine as often as necessary, with enthusiasm!

Remember, new habits take some effort to get started. You have to put some consistent energy into them. It's like pushing a large heavy ball. It takes some effort to get it started, but once it's rolling it's easy to keep going. This is the way to help yourself build the new habits and energetic patterns that can recreate the life of freedom you are seeking.

__Powerful Technique__ you can use whenever you want to redirect energy away from sexual impulses:

Inhale slowly and deeply to a count of ten, or any count that you are comfortable with (in the fresh air if possible). Tense the whole body to a count of three, then completely let go and relax all the muscles as you exhale the breath using the same count as the inhalation. Continue this exercise several times until you feel reenergized, balanced, and back in control.

This is a great energy shifter because in this process the heart and lungs act as powerful magnets that pull the energy away from the sex organs, balancing the energy in your body. It is quite simple, as you can see, but it is both powerful and effective. Try it. It works!

Chapter 14
Getting Out Of Hell

I think that hell is an appropriate topic to follow our discussions about addictions!

The dark ages concept of hell is that it is a geographic location. It is not. Hell is a state of consciousness where we suffer intensely from our separation from Truth, Joy, Divine Love, and the awareness of our soul's oneness with our Benevolent Source. The geographic element is only a natural consequence of our state of consciousness drawing us into a matching energetic matrix, whether in this world or the next. Just like we do in relationship.

Here's a marvelous little story that shows us how to get out of hellish relationships, or hellish environments or conditions of any kind. It's a story[*] of a man who flies his small plane to a conference in a nearby country. As he is flying, he sees out of the corner of his eye a rat chewing on the control cables. He knows that if he doesn't kill the rat, the plane will surely crash. But, he also realizes that he cannot let go of the controls without crashing, either. And 10,000 feet below is

_____

[*] Adapted from a story by Paramahansa Yogananda.

a rocky mountain terrain, so landing anywhere nearby is also out of the question.

Then he gets an inspiration! He puts on his oxygen mask and begins to fly higher and higher and higher. And finally as the air becomes thinner and thinner, the rat can no longer breathe. After a couple of minutes the rat rolls over and is dead! The man is then able to continue on successfully to his destination and to the rest of his life.

This is a perfect example of what we have to do. We, too, have to learn to fly higher and higher in consciousness, taking our attention and our energy away from all the rats of lower impulses and lower consciousness, and start putting it to work on our higher and more worthwhile pursuits.

It is in this scientific, energy focused way that you can regain control of your life. And what great joy comes to those who are no longer controlled by lower states of consciousness and their hellish army of bad habits and addictions. Through the process of up-leveling your consciousness comes the power to regain the kingdom of your happiness. There is no lasting happiness outside of the realm of wisdom and self-control. And creating a daily meditation practice will be of the greatest help in taking you there!

So, that's it. You just need to go within into the stillness of the Cosmic Carwash to get cleaned up, because spiritually we are all like beautiful new BMWs that are stuck in the primal mud of mortal consciousness.

I'd recommend you do that twice a day, both morning and evening, for just ten or fifteen minutes to start, and that will make all the difference in the world. When you come out the other end of your carwash-meditation, you'll find that the car of your consciousness is lookin' good and feeling much better! Believe me, there's nothing as immediately healing and deeply refreshing as what you gain from regular meditation.

Further, through the practice of regular ever-deepening meditation, you'll discover to your great relief and delight that there has been no permanent damage to your soul, no matter what physical, mental, or relationship disasters may have slammed you onto the rocks of intense suffering and despair. For we live in the realm of relativity where there are no absolutes.

Therefore, there are no unforgivable errors and no absolute losses. This is only school. And though we often have to repeat painful lessons and classes over and over again until we get them right, everyone, in time, is destined to graduate! For it is your Father's good pleasure to give you the kingdom of love and enlightenment. *"For what father whose son asketh for bread giveth a stone?"**

---

* Luke 11:11

Chapter 15
A New Masculinity

The New Age woman and man are necessarily going to be different than they were in days gone by; otherwise we'll have to call this "The Same Old Age"!

Healthy and happy individuals in any age are balanced. And though balance is very much an individual formula, there are some principles and qualities that are clearly generic and much needed as we seek to advance our humanness and thereby create better relationships and a better world.

Some of these qualities I want to mention are, first, the need for women, in general, to be able to express more fully their strength, power and wisdom; and secondly, the need for men to acknowledge the importance of integrating the qualities of unconditional love, tenderness, and compassion into their lives and relationships.

This is a wonderful time for women, and for men, too, as they come to understand it, for at last we are coming out of an imbalance that has been holding the world family back for well over a thousand years. This past Dark Age has been functioning, or perhaps better stated, "disfunctioning," as a male dominated world, one that has subjugated and abused women and given men a false sense of what their role was; and from that a grave misuse of their innate power ensued. As with any imbalance, it cannot exist indefinitely. There will always come into play universal forces that will push us toward correcting the imbalance. Thank God!

This is what's happening currently as the world's consciousness is being stimulated to upgrade our sense of who we really are. Which is, that we are all souls assigned here to learn that we are not just these limited, ego-gendered forms, but we are spiritual beings who are being asked to learn how to express more perfectly and more beautifully our essential nature.

When we understand this, we can then see that what we receive in relationship from the opposite gender is a Divinely ordained part of our learning. Without women being in their full authenticity and expressing all their unique gifts and powers, how can the world evolve to its full potential? And men cannot hope to achieve *their* own full potential without receiving the unique and indispensable gifts of love, power, and wisdom that are expressed through their feminine counterpart.

And that's because we are absolutely

indispensable to each other. Not just in the light of our biology, but also because of the unique mental, emotional, and spiritual make-up of our different natures that are gifted to us from our Universal Source. There is a tremendous amount of learning that is uniquely available to us by receiving the wisdom that is offered to us from the opposite gender.

As a result of this imbalance, many generations have passed in our current western culture that have shown us very few good examples of a higher and more fulfilling way to express our manhood. So much so that we are now left with very little in our lore and history that we can identify with to help us see where the best direction our masculinity's evolution needs to head.

In order for a man to feel whole in this world, he needs to acknowledge, nurture and express all aspects of himself. These include not only his physical, mental, sexual, and willful traits, but his emotional, spiritual, and relationship qualities, as well.

It's only when all facets of ourselves are acknowledged and integrated in a balanced and harmonious way that we can at last feel that long sought sense of wholeness. When we are in a consciousness of wholeness we live from a place of true balance and personal power where we can more fully enjoy the magnificent experience of being a man or a woman.

And, when we're feeling at our best, this is life affirming to us that we are going in the right direction. Life is telling us that what we're doing is good for us! We should pay attention to this...and its opposite!

This is, in fact, what I've been saying all along. Pay attention to your feelings. They are not just something to incidentally notice, but rather, they are clear signals from your higher self, trying to communicate with you.

There is so much we learn from the introspective practices, but there is also much that we can learn from observing nature, as well. The quality of tenderness expressed by the male in many animal species bonds and nurtures the members of its social group where it is often dominate. This in no way diminishes the male's power, authority, or his role as protector of his kind. In fact, we can easily behold that these qualities are natural to many animals and expressed as part of their wholeness.

In order for man to be in a state of wholeness, all aspects of his being need to be honored, appreciated, and encouraged to participate equally in contributing to his overall wellbeing. It's like having several software programs interacting together to successfully run our lives. If we have trouble loading or running one or more of the programs, or one of them freezes up or crashes, our life is not going to be completely successful.

Does this sound familiar? I'd be surprised if it didn't. As human beings, we all have areas to improve upon. For men, that most often is in the areas that ask us to upgrade the underdeveloped character qualities of unconditional love, tenderness, and compassion. But don't be confused that I mean anything that has to do with weakness. I do not.

If one or more parts of yourself are not being allowed to express their wisdom and gifts as part of the greater whole, then you are being less than what your higher soul nature is asking you to be, and you will have the feeling that something important is missing in your life. When you feel this way, you are not in your full power.

Sometimes we overcompensate for this by putting too much emphasis on one or more of our other qualities, not recognizing that this is just a variation on the same theme.

Balance and wholeness will naturally

express uniquely in each one of us. We each have a distinctive gift to give to the world family and it will be like no other that has ever been given. Therefore, it's imperative that you discover, and live from, the more authentic sense of who you really are, a unique ray of the Infinite Light. I encourage you to work at awakening, strengthening, and integrating the qualities that *you know* are underdeveloped in your nature.

Let's look at tenderness as an example. Most men can express some tenderness from time to time; perhaps when they pick up and hold a newborn or little child. And some easily express tenderness to their pets. But what is really being asked for is for us to expand beyond this limited expression, this segmenting of where this quality is deemed acceptable, and express it more fully in all areas of our lives.

The reason that the fuller expression of male tenderness is so far from the norm today is because this quality has to come from a place of wisdom and strength. Much like Maslow's famous *Hierarchy of Needs*, I believe there is also a hierarchy of character qualities.

Until the qualities of unconditional love and compassion are awakened and cultivated, and a strong and healthy sense of self and self-sufficiency are also dominate in the character of a man, he will not likely be interested in or able to express the still higher qualities of tenderness and compassion that are the natural result of these other qualities existing foundationally in his personality.

Being able to develop the more complete expression of male tenderness and compassion is one of the essential things our present evolutionary opportunity is asking of us. It will balance us more completely with our feminine counterparts and bring us to a place of feeling happier, safer, more peaceful, and enthusiastic about the direction our lives and relationships are headed. This is a description of how we can move toward a greater sense of wholeness, and is a cultural prerequisite for us to evolve into the higher age that is calling to us now.

To be able to climb this ladder to a fuller expression of manhood requires two indispensable ingredients. One is the knowledge of why it is of value, and two, the desire and willingness to make the effort to claim it. It is the introspective journey that alone will grant a man this higher and more satisfying state of consciousness and being.

Men too often worry about not wanting to appear too feminine, and women usually don't want to appear too masculine. However, I believe that these issues, though powerful in society, show us that many people have only a superficial and shallow understanding of the valuable differences that exist between the two sexes. Why, then, do you think so many people feel insecure and worry about these things? Beyond not wanting to have our sexual preferences mistaken, I think it is because we are not anywhere near clear or secure in who we really are, both as members of our particular gender and as souls.

We all want other people to approve of us, naturally. But we tend to follow the norms more than we think about a better way to be. Though this is definitely normal, normal does not necessarily mean it is something that will always be for our best benefit. Just because most people do something doesn't necessarily give it the gold medal stamp of universal truth and value.

So much of what we feel is based on what others think of us, or what we think they think of us. It's completely human and natural to be affected by what others think or say about us. And here we have ingrained patterns of responses, too. We can call them our defenses. We all have patterns like that. No one likes to be criticized or laughed at, for example. The feelings that come up for us when we react to personal attacks are usually not pleasant.

Though all those feelings are real and painful, they have come to us as self-generated learnings. And in the larger view, that's not bad! This is one of the important ways that we figure things out.

Because of this, we often put much of our time, energy, and emotion into doing what we think will be acceptable to the important people in our lives. This, of course, is not all bad, but in doing so we risk the possibility of being so outside of ourselves and our own truth that we miss the opportunity to discover who we really are.

We are not here just to please others! We are here in this world in order to progress toward a greater awareness of our *true* Self, the soul, and that core work is only discovered through the various forms of introspection that I've mentioned. Remember, your value to the world is far greater when you are living your life "on purpose" and in the full authentic integrity of someone who is listening and acting from their own inner guidance and knowing.

Be careful of being so busy that you don't have time for self-discovery, or of being too afraid of what you might uncover. If either of these scenarios sound at all like you, acknowledge that to continue in this way is a subtle, but real, form of self-abuse and will slow your progress in creating the relationship and life you so very much yearn for. So, affirm your courageousness and keep moving forward, ever forward!

It is now time for more men and women to stand up and be examples of the balance, beauty, and power that integrating both the masculine and feminine in our nature brings. In doing so, we will help the world family begin to feel more comfortable and informed about the value of becoming the whole, and thereby happier and more peaceful individuals that our evolution is asking each of us to be.

So, what does all this have to do with you finding the ideal partner to joyously live out the rest of your life with? The answer is... EVERYTHING! It is Universal Law that we are always going to draw an exact esoteric and energetic match to our dominate thoughts and feelings, whether they are about money issues, health or career issues, or in finding the ideal relationship.

Therefore, if you want to be in a relationship with a strong, powerful, balanced, loving, fun, caring, and tender individual, you must *be* those very things yourself first, in order to draw that type of person into your space and into your heart.

If you just want a little happiness and a little respect in this world, you can easily have that. But why would you want to settle for a pauper's portion of happiness, abundance, and love when it is your cosmic birthright to have it all? This pot of relationship gold does exist, and it has your name on it! It is, in truth, waiting for you at the end of the rainbow that *you* first create in your own consciousness and then follow with your belief in yourself, and your willingness to take the journey of self-improvement, which will build and strengthen these important qualities.

When this vision of the new you becomes so clear and powerful that it turns into your quest and your passion, you'll realize that you cannot and will not settle for being anything less than you know you can be!

Chapter 16
Gender Wisdom

"Expand your wisdom as regards gender." Okay, what does that mean? What I mean by this is when we become overly invested in all that it means to us to be a woman, or all that it means to us to be a man according to our varying cultural and personal belief systems, we take ourselves further away from the truth that we are, in fact, genderless souls.

On our *Journey to Forever* we are all moving across the grand landscape of time and space, across incarnations and different ages gathering gems of soul learning that will eventually lead us to the greatest treasure of all, our own Enlightenment! But in every landscape, in every incarnational setting, we will meet souls at different levels of soul evolution working on whatever Divinely ordained lessons may be up for them at that time. And when we have this awareness, we can then be more unconditional and inclusive in our love and compassion for all beings, and just serve them "where they are at" and respond like the great ones who "Judge not."

Furthermore, we've all been here more times than most people can even begin to imagine — thousands upon thousands of times. And in doing so, we've all played countless roles in both feminine and masculine forms.

So, when you carry this fuller understanding with you in a more conscious way, it provides you with several benefits. One, it gives you a lot more emotional breathing space to just be who you are; to lovingly and joyously accept yourself as you are right now in the middle of your colossal journey across the ages. Two, it gives you a much more wisdom-based understanding of *everyone else* you see marching across the pages of time with you. Three, what does true wisdom blossom into? It blossoms into an ever-increasing acceptance and compassion for all other beings. And four, when you are in that state of a more *inclusive* consciousness, you make the world a more peaceful and loving place for all the other souls who are journeying here with you.

Another specific benefit that this inclusive vision brings us is a healthier and more holistic understanding of the gay community in the light of its own truth and naturalness. In this broader and deeper perception, the gay community comes into a much clearer focus.

Many of today's gay people are souls that are just now in the early stages of changing gender, often after having spent many recent lifetimes as the opposite sex. And now it's time for their life's lessons to shift their focus to new learnings that are better experienced in the opposite biology.

And of course, as people make these transitions there are strong subconscious memories and connections with the experiences, choices, and relationships of the past that were natural to their previous gender. Thus, here again we can see the great wisdom from the enlightened ones who always counsel us to "Judge ye not."

The deeper we go into any introspective arena, the more we discover that correspondingly our vision of life continues to expand in scope, beauty, intelligence, and wonder, giving us ever greater perceptions and joy. Greater by far than those offered by what our present day culture proclaims as truth, or even what the sum total of all the religious teaching have offered us across the centuries. And, I gratefully acknowledge that they each have offered us much, indeed.

Yet, the ultimate answers are not contained in any theology exam or in any belief structure, doctrine or dogma, but rather they are uncovered through the direct attainment of an ever-expanding enlightened state that only comes after lifetimes of spiritual effort and evolution.

On an even grander scale, when looked at as the whole of humanity, there is another great shift happening in our time that is helping our world evolve into a more balanced state. It is, at long last, that the Divine Feminine aspect of Spirit is coming back into power, and back into balance with the Divine Masculine, for without a balance of these two aspects of Spirit manifesting within us, both individually and collectively in our world, we will continue to find ourselves feeling incomplete and out of harmony with Life and Truth. In fact, accomplishing this balance is a great and absolutely necessary step forward for every soul as they continue to peel the onion of ignorance from both their minds and their hearts.

An important piece of our evolutionary journey requires that we learn to integrate the valuable qualities that each gender expresses. Why do you think we have to have so many incarnations in both genders? In this context, that becomes completely clear. We are here to learn to be all that we can and eventually will be.

In order to do that we must embody all the highest qualities and virtues that are the best expressions of our total humanness. Look at all the greatest souls who have ever walked this earth. What do we see? We see the most sublime tenderness and love perfectly mixed with the boundless strength and power to fully live their lives according to the truths that they came here to model for us.

All the important qualities of humility, self-control, love, tenderness, strength of character, willpower, purity, wisdom, and non-attachment need to be developed, refined, and polished into the best and most beautiful expression of you that Spirit intends. And built into the soul's evolutionary intent is the divine support system that is ever intelligently and compassionately offering you an endless stream of opportunities to accomplish every good thing you are striving for, including the soul fulfilling relationship you are questing after. You *will* be able to access all of this by the right use of your free will, and by exercising the quality of complete willingness to continue learning and growing in all areas of your life.

In this moment in history, the truth is that we have collectively been struggling for a long time to leave a very dark age behind. And though most people are not yet consciously sensitive to the gradual, but profound, vibrational changes that each one of us contributes to on this plane, these growing positive forces of our evolving consciousness are now beginning to tip the scale of our earth back toward the positive, back toward the light. These positive changes in consciousness are at last beginning to outweigh the effect of those who have long been in varying degrees of fearful and negative consciousness.[*]

This positive response to the pull of Spirit's evolutionary intentions is at last moving us into a higher age; and thereby has created a great spiritual opportunity for those that choose, through their willingness, to embrace the magnetic up-leveling pull of Spirit. Through this quality of willingness you can quickly put yourself in harmony with the positive forces in the universe and aid in accelerating not only your own soul's evolution, but powerfully contribute to the sum total of the evolution of our world.

It is right now that we have an unparalleled opportunity to advance everything our souls have been longing for. The joy and wisdom that will be its fruits will unfold a new and better you that can then draw and enter into a relationship that, until now, you dared not even dream of!

---

[*] See recommended reading: *Power vs. Force* by David R. Hawkins M.D. PhD

Chapter 17
Increasing Your Personal Magnetism

I had an amazing, life-altering experience a couple of years ago. I had gone to hear an inspirational talk that was to be followed by a one-hour group meditation. As I took my seat near the back of the room, I recognized a man up near the front on the opposite side. I had not seen or spoken to this man for nearly ten years, and remembered him as a really nice man whom I'd always gotten along well with. His wife had been a close friend of my ex-wife for many years.

While I was going through that very difficult divorce about twelve years ago, he happened to run into me, gave me a one-liner criticism, and walked on. So, being the sensitive creature that I am, seeing him brought that old criticism back to my mind and to my feelings.

After the inspiring talk I began to settle into the meditation, but my mind would not quiet down to my interiorizing intentions. It was busy running scenarios about how I was going to justify and defend myself about the past if I got a chance to talk to this man after the meditation. Not only that, I was thinking about what I would share with him about my wonderful and successful new life in recent years. I was clearly wanting him to think well of me, to be impressed with what I would share with him.

As I sat there then in the meditation, watching my thoughts as the silent observer, I realized that this was something that I'd done for as long as I could remember, in one form or another, defending myself or striving to impress others. Realizing that was a jaw dropping awakening. I didn't like what I was just discovering about myself, either! So, what could I do to remedy this no longer useful pattern?

Then the voice from deep within said, "You have nothing to defend and no one to impress." As this new thought kept repeating itself, "You have nothing to defend and no one to impress," its healing truth began to dawn on me. I really didn't need to defend my actions or myself. I was and am clear and content within my own conscience. I knew that I had behaved honorably under those difficult circumstances. The only thing I needed to be now was my own authentic self! Nothing more or less than who I am at this point in time.

As for the "impressing others" part, though we all want to be well thought of, in this situation the inner voice was pointing out to me that these thoughts were coming from a mental and emotional tape that was based upon not thinking I was good enough as I am; that this was an expression of insecurity and low self esteem.

Wow, I thought, *that's exactly why I was doing that! And I'm really comfortable now in choosing to let these two old tapes go away! They no longer represent the evolving and more conscious and healthier me. Indeed, the only thing I need to be is my own authentic self! Nothing more or less than who I am at this point in time.*

I am a child of the Most High, equal to and valued as much as everyone else; not a quarter inch more or less than anyone else. We are all souls struggling to uncover the fullness of our own value and divinity and I'm only required to be who I am right now.

Wonderful! Freeing! Amazing! And so obvious, once I uncovered what I was really doing. So, with that greatly cleaned up, I was then able to move more deeply, quietly, and happily into my meditation.

After the meditation a buffet lunch was served. As I got my plate filled and turned around, with whom did I have immediate eye contact? Yep, you guessed it. So, I went and joined my old acquaintance with the clean intention to enjoy our conversation and catch up on each other's last ten years in a loving and interested way, without any ego agendas.

Can you imagine how our lunch together went? Yep, you're right again. We had a really good connection and the feeling I got from him as I left for another appointment was that he had truly enjoyed himself, and that he was happily surprised that he did!

Now, why do you suppose I felt that additional surprise energy coming from him? I believe that it was because he didn't feel any undercurrent of my wanting to defend or to impress. All he felt was my genuine love and interest in him.

I had a miracle that day, and I'm sharing it with you because I think it touches a universal truth. "You, too, have nothing to defend and no one to impress." **"You have nothing to defend and no one to impress."** At your core, you and I are <u>already</u> good enough. Your job now is to get more in touch with this and the many other eternal truths that await your discovery deep within your sacred self.

But you might ask, "Aren't there times when it's appropriate to defend yourself and others?" Obviously, yes, there are. Are there also times when it's fitting to share your successes and to do your best to make a good impression? Again, yes there are. But to spend *all* your time within your mind, constantly running offensive and defensive tapes, keeps you in an agitated state of insecurity, and that blocks you from experiencing the healing and nurturing connection with Spirit that is always available to you just behind your noisy mind in the deeper quietness of your soul.

Remember this. The power that lights the stars is the same power that lights your soul, and it awaits your discovery behind all the fears and foibles that try to block your way. So, it is here that we see the priceless value of discovering what our inner challenges are, because once these no longer useful patterns are identified we can then consciously choose to replace them with healthier ones. This not only calms us and makes us feel better, but opens the way to a deeper communion that can only be accessed in the all nurturing stillness that lies hidden just behind the restless mind.

It is through introspective processes like these that we can rapidly up-level our consciousness and make for much more meaningful and enjoyable interactions with others — especially that special one who is destined to partner with you during this part of your colossal journey across the ages.

Can you see what this story has to do with increasing your personal magnetism? I think that you can. Everyone obviously wants to be around someone who is genuinely interested in them and cares about them. And this has an underpinning of universal truth. Which is, *your personal magnetism increases or decreases in direct proportion to your interest in, caring for, and unconditionally loving of other people.*

Chapter 18
Equality

My core agenda coming back from my year-plus of prayer and meditation in the forest in southern Oregon in 1999 and 2000 was that the relationship I was deeply seeking, and the only one that I would accept, would have to be one that was completely equal. I'll illustrate this idea of equality for you by contrasting it with a brief story.

From the superb movie, *The Joy Luck Club,* comes the tale of four Chinese mothers and their four daughters. The mothers, having all come from a different country, generation, and culture than their daughters, create expectations and tensions that challenge the relationships they each have with their daughters. Each one of these eight women in her own way is struggling to discover a more authentic expression of herself, and through that create a breakthrough that will lead them to a happier and more fulfilling life.

One of the four daughters marries a businessman who ends up being very much like her damaged mother, emotionally unavailable. Together the couple decides to be equal in everything to do with money. So, they make lists and argue over who pays for the flea medicine for "your" cat, and "I don't think it's fair to have to pay for your ice cream that I never eat." And so on. This drives the young wife totally nuts!

The good news is that by facing up to what this pain is telling her, it stimulates both the wife and her mother to initiate positive changes that dramatically improve each of their lives and the relationship they have together, and, incidentally, leaves the husband clueless and divorced.

By contrast, I want you to understand that this is *not* the type of equality I want to illuminate for you! The type of equality that I want to focus on is based in unconditional love, trust, and thoughtfulness.

In this context, *Equality* is another one of my holy words. Holy because it can bring you a stunningly beautiful and unparalleled gift that cannot be delivered to your address by any other means.

For man and woman to reach their full potential, they each need to partake of the wisdom and vision of *the intimate other* in order to find their wholeness. When we view a scene with just one eye, then the other, each view is slightly different. But when the scene is viewed with both eyes the object being looked at takes on a more three dimensional nature, which is a truer interpretation of its reality.

A hologram is another good analogy. A hologram allows us to look at, and often through, things from every possible direction. This is the gift that is available to us when we've developed the balance of both the masculine and feminine qualities in our nature; and in successful relationships a healthy environment of equality is paramount to being able to develop, nurture, and expand these higher perceptions and character traits.

In order for a plant to grow, blossom, and fruit into the optimum beauty and expression that is unique to its kind, the environment it lives in also needs to be optimum for this to be achieved. So it is in relationship.

When each partner is treated fully as an equal, and honors the efforts, challenges, and dreams of their loved one by offering them encouragement, enthusiasm, support, and a feeling of being safe and unjudged, then they have given their partner an ideal environment in which to love, learn, grow, and prosper.

The environment in this type of relationship can then truly become a heaven on earth! This is an example of the full and higher expression of equality I want to illumine for you, one that is excited, rather than threatened, by the brave and creative growth efforts of their one most cherished.

When we live in a chronic consciousness of fear, energetically more fear is being invited to move in, and this can spiral us down into a miserable state of despair. But when we choose to live in a state of willingness, hope, love, and joy, no matter what comes along to knock us off our horse, we naturally draw to us more and more of what we are. And when your partner is positively intended in a like manner, you are rich beyond measure. This is the way life in relationship can be for those who catch the vision of its unbounded potential and make the effort to bring it into reality in their own unique life.

You can see the theme of this entire book on creating an ideal relationship is really all about learning to live life in a more conscious and positive co-creative manner. It is a simple concept, but it requires both an inner strength and willingness to continuously keep working at improving the patterns of your thoughts, feelings, and behaviors.

Deepening your understanding of the value and importance of *Equality* in relationship will help you to dramatically expand the abundant space in your heart where you are inviting your beloved partner to take up residence. And when *you* make the effort to offer this higher level of love and acceptance to another soul, you will find that the rewards are both magical and wonderfully abundant!

Chapter 19
Beyond Religion Is Divine Relationship

A brisk sea breeze greeted him just as the morning sun was beginning to ease its way over the monastery wall. Giving little notice to the all too familiar miracle, the Dominican priest hurried across the courtyard toward the chapel. He knew that immediately after Mass he would be diving back into his work on the third part of his colossal ***Summa Theologiae,*** which so far had consumed six years of his life.

As perhaps the greatest mind of his time, what Thomas Aquinas couldn't have known that morning was that when he would step out of the chapel there in Naples some two hours, hence he would not write one more word. For on that early December 6th morning in 1273, the "Prince of Scholastics" had such an epiphany, such a life altering, mystical experience, that never again would he have any interest in intellectuality and the doctrines and dogmas it cultures. He said, "Such things have been revealed to me that now all I have written appears in my eyes as of no greater value than straw!"*

So, it was through this ecstatic, mystical experience that Thomas Aquinas's consciousness moved dramatically away from the linear, never satisfied, ego based realm of the mind and into the all-satisfying realm of soul awareness. In the twinkling of an eye, Thomas Aquinas stepped out of the limited territory of reason and into the vast, all-satisfying sphere of direct perception.

Yet man, in his reasoning, left-brain dominated consciousness always seems to get caught up in the same cosmic error, again and again, age after age. He thinks that his reasoning *thoughts* about God are giving him actual *knowledge* of God.

But the flaw is obvious. For our left-brain is nothing but a processor. It reasons and analyzes. It functions by deduction, by inference, not by true firsthand experience. And so man gets himself into all kinds of mischief by relying too heavily on the imperfect tool of his intellect.

"The world is flat" and "the sun orbits the earth" are a couple of useful examples of the

---

* **Summma Theologiae** was intended as a manual for religious beginners. Its purpose was to provide a compilation of all of the main theological teachings of that time. Today, in its original unfinished form, it comprises some sixty volumes and totals well over 10,000 pages.

mischief this lesser tool can get us into.

But interestingly, when we listen to the enlightened ones from across the ages, they always speak about their *direct experiences*, not about their reasoning thoughts!

This next story really brings this point home. In her stunning book, *My Stroke of Insight: A Brain Scientist's Personal Journey,* Dr. Jill Taylor consciously watches the hemorrhaging left hemisphere of her brain fill with blood and shut down. At the same time she perceives her consciousness moving over into the right side of her brain where she experiences, without any religious overlay, an intensely blissful awareness of an all-satisfying love and peace. And in the absence of her reasoning, ego driven left hemisphere, she perceives herself as absolutely perfect, whole, and beautiful just the way she is.

Through the shutting down of the ever-active linear, judging side of the brain, Dr. Taylor's consciousness shifts into her right hemisphere where she experiences a powerful sense of peace and contentment, discovering there that she is not alone, and that she is "One with the universe" and one with her Source. In doing so, she accomplishes what yogis and meditators the world over know as the foundational key to spiritual discovery. She quiets the ever-busy reasoning side of her brain.

What an unexpected and amazing gift Dr. Taylor gives to the world by recounting her experience in the language and understanding of a brain scientist. In a very thorough way she gives a physiological explanation of a spiritual experience. This is such a timely gift for an age that is rapidly moving away from intellectual doctrines and dogmas and toward quantifiable personal experience.

In a recent interview on *National Public Radio*, Dr. Taylor said from her unique first person experience that: *"Religion is the left brain's story about the right brain's experience."* How wonderfully succinct is that?!

Chapter 20
The Dark Side's Complaint

On a morning very much like today our ever-effulgent, all-powerful, life-giving sun got a text message from the Heavenly Father requiring him to report immediately to His spacious office. Obeying the Divine summons, our beloved sun wondered what this might be all about.

He didn't have to wait long before the Omnipotent One appeared before him. "My sun, it is always a joy to greet you. But today I must tell you that I have received a serious complaint against you. I've heard from *the darkness of night* that you are eternally chasing him, harassing him, and not giving him even a moment's peace! What do you have to say for yourself, my sun?"

"Revered Father, I do not know what to say. I confess I must be very ignorant for I have never even heard of *the darkness of night.* So, I implore you, Blessed Father, that you ask him to join us here immediately so that I may apologize."

Well, as you no doubt quickly surmised, our dear sun never did get to apologize to his accuser. For light and dark cannot exist in the same space at the same time, and more importantly for our purposes we need to remember that light and dark cannot exist in the same consciousness at the same time, either!

Which one is more powerful, Light or Darkness? Put them together and find out. Light wins every time! And it's the same in Love vs. Hate. Love is the greater power.

So, if you want to win your soul's battle for freedom from darkness and ignorance, you must join with the divine forces of Love and Light that are waiting for you to call them forth out of the secret temple that lies hidden behind the restlessness of your mind.

It is the two-sided gift of *free will* that both makes us gods, and gives us license to run the car of our life ignorantly into the ditch of dark suffering. Of course, no one in their right mind would consciously choose pain and suffering over joy, health, and wisdom — which only leads me to conclude that most of us are *not* in our right minds! This is so blatantly clear that it is completely undeniable.

So, here's the applicable point for us. After we have suffered enough here in the cosmic reform school, we call out to our Creator for relief. And that immediately brings us help, in the form of insights and guidance, that begins to awaken wisdom and understanding in our consciousness. If you're really adamant about connecting your life with the Divine Relief, Spirit is constrained to respond to all such sincere and heartfelt pleas. For The Divine is not only the Father, but the Mother as well. And what in all creation is more tender, loving, compassionate, and unconditional than the Divine under the form of the Universal Mother? Always remember that Spirit can respond to you in any form or quality that pulls at your unique heart. For Who do you think put that unique feeling there in the first place? This reveals an even deeper truth. The Divine Beloved wants your love more than *you* want Hers, Its, or His.

So, on this colossal journey across the ages your natural desires for a better and more fulfilling life are most easily and directly supported and accomplished when you connect your consciousness and your life with your Loving Source. Establishing that connection with the very One who has become you is the key underlying accomplishment that will move you to the next giant leap forward in your spiritual evolution, and make you fit for drawing yourself into much higher forms and expressions of relationship.

This does not mean that I am encouraging you to embrace any particular religion. Rather, I am encouraging you to develop a relationship with the Divine Beloved directly. If following a particular doctrine helps you to get where you want to go, that's fine. But remember, it's not the doctrine you want to embrace, but the Beloved who is already in your heart awaiting your discovery.

So always remember, it never was, and never will be, about the name over the door; rather, it will always be about the relationship that you nurture within your own heart and consciousness.

And, you might ask, how does all this directly relate to you "avoiding marrying a toad"? When you get in touch with your soul nature as a ray of the universal love, light, wisdom, and joy, those qualities will begin to dominate your consciousness more and more, and then *spill over and flow out into all the actions and interactions of your unique life.*[*] And because everything has both an energetic and magnetic essence, you will naturally draw to yourself those who resonate with your new, higher, and purer level of love, power, wisdom, and goodness!

---

[*] *Neither do men light a candle, and put it under a bushel, but on a candlestick, and it gives light unto all...* Matthew 5:15

Chapter 21
Planning Your Escape!

We are each a prisoner living within the boundary walls of our own limited beliefs. Change and expand your perceptions and beliefs and you have changed and expanded the boundaries of your world and the experiences you will have in it.

In Henri Charrière's famous story, *Papillon,* he tells the true story of how, as a petty criminal in France, he was convicted of a murder he didn't commit and then sentenced to a penal colony in French Guiana on Devil's Island just off the northeastern coast of South America.

Papillon tried constantly to escape from this notoriously brutal prison, only to be recaptured again and again, each time having his prison time extended; and at one point being put in solitary confinement for two and a half years.

Finally, more than twenty years later, he was allowed to "retire" to a lonely and inescapable part of the prison-island located several miles off the South American coast. There, on a cliff hundreds of feet above the violent waves that unendingly pounded the rocky cliffs, Papillon continued focusing on his undying dream of escaping to a new and better life. Every day he imagined himself floating safely across the twenty-four miles of open ocean to the South American mainland, and there finding a way back to the life he had dreamed of for so long.

After months of pondering how he might escape from the inescapable, he began to notice that the waves that constantly crashed against the base of the cliffs, making it impossible to jump and swim without being smashed to death on the jagged rocks, actually had a measurable rhythm. He noticed that with a predictable regularity, about every seven sets of waves, there was a moment where the waves and the sea seemed to retreat from their pattern and actually create a current that went away from the shore for just a few seconds. Perhaps this would be just enough time to allow him to get clear of the crashing waves that would otherwise smash him mercilessly upon the rocks; provided, of course, that he first survived the jump of several hundred feet!

Papillon decided that this was his long-sought chance for freedom. He would seize it to try to escape one last time. So, he began gathering dry coconut shells, which he carefully sewed into a canvas bag about three feet square. When the day he had chosen finally arrived, he perched himself on the edge of the cliff, watching and confirming the patterns of the waves over and over again.   When he was sure it was the exact moment for the sea to flow outwards again, he threw his float bag into the sea and jumped off the cliff.

When his head popped back up out of the water he saw that it was just as he'd hoped, the sea had begun to retreat from the cliff for the few precious seconds that he needed!   Frantically, he swam to retrieve his coconut filled bag. Laying his body across his handmade life bag, he paddled furiously away from the jagged rocks. He was just barely able to clear the raging surf and head out into the open ocean.   Then, half swimming and half floating, he was able to navigate the twenty-plus miles westward, finally arriving on the sandy mainland shore. He was free! He'd done it! At last he had fulfilled his dream and reached his long sought freedom!

So, even after twenty pain-filled years in prison, Papillon's spirit had not been broken. He never gave up on his dream for freedom, even though he'd failed countless times before. And when we consider that his circumstances had been so extreme in their effort to keep him chained to a life that he did not want, it's truly amazing that he never gave up. His example is a clear lesson for us all.

In spite of the constant, ongoing daily opposition to his desire, Papillon was able to keep alive his faith in himself, his dream, and his underlying trust in the justice of life until at last he was able to break free of the old patterns that had ruled his days and replace them with the ones that he'd yearned for all those many long and pain-filled years.

Please take note of what Papillon focused on, and what he didn't focus on. Did he just sit up there on the cliff thinking, *Those cruel guards, those money hungry bounty hunters, that sadistic warden, that incompetent judge, they all were so evil and uncaring. They ruined my life. There's no way that I deserve to be treated like this*, and on and on?

I'm sure he didn't. He must have spent the dominant part of his time, energy, and passion focusing on what would bring him the joy he wanted to experience. His freedom!

And that's the crucial point. We get what we put our attention on. Now I'd like you to focus for a moment on the *joy* he must have felt when he gained his freedom. When we accomplish something we always feel a sense of satisfaction, don't we? And if we achieve something that's really important to us, we feel really good!

Yet, it's interesting to note that it's not so much the condition or the thing that we outwardly desire that gives us this joy. We actually experience this joy within our minds.

Let me prove it to you. If you knew there was a brand new BMW, paid for by a secret admirer and registered in your name, sitting in your driveway or parking place right now, you'd probably feel a lot of joy about that great gift. If that car were sitting there under the same conditions without you knowing about it, you wouldn't feel any joy. The owning of the car in and of itself then has absolutely no power to give you joy. The *belief* that you have about how you will feel when certain conditions are met gives you the mental permission to feel that joy, and you feel all that in your mind!

Several years ago Arnold Schwarzenegger starred in the wild and crazy science fiction film, *Total Recall,* where he went to a travel agency and bought a vacation trip to Mars. He then sat in a chair, put on the special hood and had the "virtual experience" of going to Mars. He experienced it all right inside of his mind!

The point I'd like to highlight here is that I think we don't usually notice that what we're seeking is a feeling. And that the "thing" we desire is only the vehicle, the condition, actually, that we put on our consciousness about allowing ourselves to experience that joy. Once we attain our goal we allow ourselves to have the feeling that we're desiring. That's why saints and mystics have long said that we can *choose* to be happy right now, regardless of our outer conditions.

Well, I'm pretty sure most of you haven't completely mastered that yet. I know I haven't. But I bring up this rather lofty concept because it gives us a valuable clue on how we can get in the express lane emotionally when we find ourselves stuck in the traffic of unpleasant circumstances.

Each of us has the power to be happy now. We've always had the innate power to shift our attention away from something that is unpleasant and to put it on a thought that is more enjoyable; and we do that by what we *choose* to focus our minds upon. And if you recall, in the beginning I shared the technique of *"that's not me"* that I use to nullify any negative thought or feeling that comes up for me. The reason it works so beautifully is that no thought can remain dominant in our consciousness unless we give it energy in the form of our attention.

The more you can train yourself to focus on keeping your mind and feelings in a state of happiness, independent of the ever-changing nature of outer conditions, the better. This can be a huge step forward in moving you away from the false idea that you are a victim of your circumstances. The result of even a small shift in this direction brings with it the incomparable gifts of a happier and more powerful you!

This leads us right back to your goal of a loving and deeply satisfying relationship, where, in order to accomplish this wonderful goal and fulfill your dreams you must first escape from the prison house of those old mental patterns that no longer serve your healthy goals and your evolving self.

When the dark side tricks us into running our old tapes, tapes that focus the majority of our attention on what is wrong and what we don't like in our lives and relationships, it only gives the negative side of life increasing amounts of energy and power to keep us stuck in these painful patterns. Therefore, too much focus upon the negatives in our lives and relationships only brings more of what we're really trying to avoid. Pain!

So, learn to spend time daily within your mind purposefully building new mental patterns and habits that will help you focus your attention and your energy on what you want and what you know will be good for you. This will take the energy and power away from the dark side and help power you in the right direction of fulfilling your heart's worthy desires. This is the positive, wisdom guided way of living, and is the only way you can fulfill both your sacred dreams and your destiny!

Chapter 22
Tamerlane and the Ant

With dried blood and dirt in his mouth, he dared breathe only the quietest of breaths as he lay frozen midst the stone rubble. Only a partial wall now remained, which sheltered him from the many enemy eyes that were still slowly picking their way through the corpse-strewn battlefield in search of stragglers. If he could continue to stay undiscovered for perhaps one more hour, he just might be able to steal away under the cloak of the approaching darkness.

It was just then that he saw her, only a few inches from his grounded face. Like a colossal god of power, with strength beyond imagining relative to her size, she hoisted the prize, 50 times her body weight, over her head and began the vertical climb straight up the wall.

After gaining only a few hard fought inches, nature's laws uncaringly slammed her back down into the dust. Undeterred, the tiny ant retrieved her colossal kernel of corn and attacked the wall a second time. Up she went, tenaciously battling and staggering for each unwilling inch. But down she fell again.

Again and again she fell. Again and again

she picked up her treasure and made for the unrelenting wall. By now he was mesmerized by the unshakable will of his miniature companion. He began counting. Eleven! Twenty-three! Forty times! It was beyond anything he could ever have imagined. And yet, there she was, still going at it, and against an obviously impossible set of circumstances.

An hour passed and the sun was now beginning to release its reign over the central Asian sky. But on she went. Sixty times! Sixty-nine times! And then it happened. On her seventieth try she didn't fall. She defied gravity, and man's disbelief, and pushed her prize up onto the top of the wall just as the last rays of the sun reflected golden light from her hard-earned treasure. In the next instant she was gone. She was down the other side and away to her self-made destiny!

The intensity of everything Tamerlane had experienced that day burned like a fire in his mind, from the searing defeat to the cold breath of death blowing over him. Yet, in that state of heightened awareness, the tiny little ant with her golden kernel of corn provided the greatest lesson that the great warrior would take from this battlefield. Perseverance.

Tamerlane now knew that Perseverance

was the golden key to his future. He had seen its power with his own eyes. Regrouping after this defeat, and a number of others that life would deal him, Tamerlane would eventually go on to conquer huge portions of his fourteenth century world, which included vast areas of western and central Asia, eventually founding the Timurid Dynasty that would endure for over four hundred years as the Mughal Empire of India!

And that's a great lesson for us all. Perseverance is one of the most vital keys to your self-evolution and the successful accomplishment of every desire in your heart. Just think about this power of fortitude, tenacity, and determination in this lowly ant. Stunning!

Yet, we see this quality of perseverance expressed everywhere in nature, from the ocean's unrelenting pounding on rocky shores, to its many expressions in plants, animals, and finally in mankind.

Does it seem as obvious to you, as it does to me, that The Universal Intelligence is giving us constant demonstrations of how each of us can fulfill our worthwhile desires? Life is trying to teach each of us that we must first build our psychological and spiritual muscles so that we learn how to persevere in our efforts for as long as may be necessary in order to achieve our worthy goals.

With the power of our unbreakable resolve we will gain the staying power we need to take ourselves forward over all the unseen mountains of soul learning that yet lie ahead, and through all the swamps of errors, bad habits, disbelief, and indifference, until at last we conquer the final enemy, our ego, and emerge the Soul victor of all that our life is asking of us!

This universal principle of perseverance is necessary for your journey to your idyllic and fulfilling relationship, as well, because in this dualistic world every worthwhile endeavor is challenged. But if your will is strong and your heart and mind are unwavering, you will not only be able to stay the course and achieve your goal, but you will emerge as a stronger and wiser person for having had the faith and courage to persevere.

And unlike the never satisfied Tamerlane, the treasure you will gain from conquering your lower nature and replacing it with beautiful soul qualities will in time not only draw to you a high and magnificent relationship, but your newly awakened soul qualities will outlast the very stars and be with you forevermore.

Chapter 23
How To Measure Your Progress

Are you predominately an actor or a re-actor? Happy, self-determined, and successful people consciously, willfully, and powerfully *choose* the course of their thoughts, their feelings, and their resultant actions. I call these people self-empowered conscious actors.

When we are predominately re-actors to everything that life brings to us we are not acting from our higher, more authentic and spiritually empowered self. This is an example of that old lower ego expression we've talked a lot about, victim consciousness.

One good measurement of your progress is to see to what degree you are either an actor or re-actor by looking at your compulsive patterns and negative habits versus wisdom guided thoughts and actions. Do you see improvement in these areas?

How are you doing with your interactions with others? How are others responding to you after you have instituted some of these useful new habits and patterns we've discussed? If you are working to change on the inside where it really counts, then people will begin to notice it on the outside, too.

An interesting point here, too, is not everyone will be a fit with the new evolving you anymore. Some friends and acquaintances will go away and new ones that better match the new you will appear. This is a good and valuable indicator of positive progress.

Another indicator is how you feel about yourself. Is your love, compassion, and comfortableness with yourself improving? If you're doing your inner work, it really will!

Additionally, how does the world and life look to you now? What are your new views of other people, groups, cultures, and religions? Are they the same, or are they becoming more expanded, inclusive and compassionate?

All those things are indicators of an up-leveling consciousness. And all of the above leads us to the best indicator of all. Joy! So, if you find yourself becoming increasingly happy and feeling more empowered, enthusiastic, and positive about your life, and having more trust, faith, and connection with Spirit, then these feelings are convincing to your very core that your life is connected to your Source and all is well.

Learning to be a healthy actor on the stage of life will help you to live and work from a higher set of character qualities. Then these up-leveled character traits will create new, higher, and stronger patterns of exemplary behavior that naturally draw higher-level interactions and relationships, and will also help uplift the consciousness of all those you interact with.

It is in these ways that you naturally achieve increasing levels of joy, peace, and power as an instrument of good in this world — bringing with it the knowledge that you're doing your part in making this a better and more beautiful world for all!

Chapter 24
Out of the Pond

Early in the last century, a reporter went to interview the world-renowned humanitarian, Dr. Albert Switzer, at his hospital for the poor in Africa. The journalist asked what the great humanitarian thought was mankind's greatest problem.

Expecting some deep and expansive discourse on social ills, he was surprised by the great humanist's brief and pointed answer. Dr. Switzer replied, *"Man doesn't think!"*

In a superficial sense, of course, we are thinking all the time. But about life, its cause and purpose, and how to fulfill it, these thoughts go mostly unconsidered by billions of people in our world today.

The point is, once you *do* realize that you're in the driver's seat of your life, any and all miracles are possible by your own co-creative hand, including the creation of the relationship you've long been aching for.

I hope you're starting to actually see the unlimited power you have right within you. As you begin to become conscious of this, it can feel like a new and glorious dawn, like none other you've ever experienced, and you will then sit in a stunned and appreciative silence at the magnitude of this gift and its importance to you and to all of mankind. Such is the power of a focused mind and a committed heart. So, it all comes down to what you truly want and what efforts you are willing to put forth to make your dreams your reality.

Now that we've looked at relationship from several different vantage points, let's put all of that into a larger perspective. If you recall, in the beginning I gave you the visual idea of your life being like an infinite dark wall, and by you gaining various insights and learnings, you create new openings in the wall that give you more and more understanding of life and your place in it.

Well, now it's time to step back and look at that wall, your life, as a whole. The holistic view I want you to see is that *all* of life is "relationship"! It is *how* you relate to all of your life's experiences that determines the quality, extent, and depth of the learning, growth, and self-improvement that you will gain. In a phrase, *"Life is an Attitude Ballgame."*

And because most of you picked up this book with the intent of avoiding marrying a toad — that is, you wanted to be in a healthier and more fulfilling relationship — you can now see that absolutely everything you think, do, and feel impacts your half of what you bring to that desired relationship. It is that, in total, which makes you who you are and determines energetically and magnetically who is drawn to you in relationship.

Further, we both know that you would never have picked up this book, no matter how cute those toads are on the cover, if you had not been keenly aware of the extreme pain that many of us experience in unsuccessful and unhappy relationships. You, and every one of us, clearly want to avoid pain. It's natural to the human condition, and that desire is there for a reason. It's our warning system. Pain constantly warns us when we start heading in the wrong direction.

But that's only half of the story. The other side of that coin is joy! And what joy is telling you is that you are going in the *right* direction!

Everything we do is based upon avoiding pain and striving to feel joy, bliss, and love. So the avoidance of pain and the attainment of joy, bliss, and love are the core motivations and goals of every human being. And this cannot be attained outside of living in accord with the universal laws of creation.

Because your soul is unique and absolutely

unlike any other, your journey will have its own special story and its own beautiful and romantic expressions. But for you to find your full and unique expression, both in relationship and in all the other facets of your soul's evolutionary journey, you will need to become increasingly knowledgeable and intimate with all the generic laws of life that are relentlessly driving your evolution toward your ultimate enlightenment and fulfillment. Then more and more joy, strength, and wisdom will light your way toward your goal of unending and unbroken happiness.

When you learn to remodel your life from the inside out by learning to commune with your Loving Source, you are then not so much affected by the ever-changing circumstances of life in the cosmic movie. Instead, you find that you have a portable sanctuary you can take with you everywhere you go. And this tangible awareness of the indwelling Spirit then acts as a Divine Light of protection for you as you move forward through all the chapters of this life.

Nonetheless, though it is always with you, it is ever *your* job to remain conscious and connected. When you forget, darkness comes in, but as soon as you remember, the light instantly dispels the darkness again.

So, this is the most critical lesson and habit

to instill in your consciousness; that of staying connected to your Source. And the most direct and powerful way that you can build that power to stay unbroken in the embrace of the *inner relationship* is to create the habit of regular daily meditation.[*]

---

[*] "Be still and know that I Am God." Psalms 46:10

Chapter 25
The Greatest Secret!

Many years ago I was in a relationship that provided me with a number of valuable lessons. All of those relationship lessons are still quite vivid and appreciated by me today, in large part because they were delivered by the blowtorch of pain.

The metaphorical description of that relationship went like this. Not feeling I was powerful enough or valuable enough to myself, or others, I thereby chose the role of the spiritual martyr in the relationship, and hence accepted the pain and suffering that naturally came with those ignorant choices. Metaphorically lying down in the road of this relationship triggered a natural response in the emotionally wounded software of my partner. Which was, "Road kill! Yeah!"

Seeing that, she would then jump in her psychic car and practice driving back and forth over me. Now, who was at fault here, the Pavlovian driver, or the idiot lying in the road? The answer, of course, is both and neither. Both, because each was 100% responsible for their own behavior. And neither, because these were just the natural results that came from making ignorant choices outside of the protecting umbrella of true knowledge and wisdom. One of wisdom's greatest insights is that it's not about blame. But rather, it's more about learning from pain's gifts.

From this we can begin to see why life offers us pain in response to our choices, because sometimes that's the only thing that will get the message through to us. Pain does not come to destroy us, but to point us in a healing direction. After that, it's always about our next choice, and the next, and the next.

Accordingly, as long as we *choose,* consciously or subconsciously, to continue living under the delusive spell of *victim consciousness,* we will continue to draw people and circumstances into our lives to help us fulfill these ignorant victim based beliefs.

Of course, most people don't realize they're putting out a flag with "victim" written on it. But these subconscious beliefs will definitely reveal themselves through the partners you draw, if you're willing to look.

And so here it is, one last time. Life will deliver you partners and conditions that match your vision and your level of consciousness. It is the unalterable law of the universe.

If you truly want to live your life with a powerful, loving, considerate, nurturing, and angelic being, and you are willing to do the evolutionary work I've illustrated for you, then you've just described your destiny! Now all that remains is for you to take the journey that I've just outlined for you in this book.

As we conclude our journey together, the greatest secret I can share with you is *that* which you are seeking...you already are! The journey to the ideal relationship is a sacred part of the vaster journey that leads to the realization that we are each an expression of our Benevolent and Loving Source. As such, we are each endowed with all the infinite bounty of love, wisdom, power, and joy that are inherent in our Creator.

It is Spirit that has become all things and all persons. And in the cosmic movie theater of creation, Spirit has projected the ideas of individuation onto the screen of time and space. In this colossal play, He watches how His "free will" expressions, you and I, are progressing across the centuries, before we ultimately discover the longed for treasure right within ourselves.

Therefore, the journey, and the quest of all of life, is to rediscover our true spiritual nature that has temporarily taken up residence in these mortal forms. As you begin to unearth your true spiritual identity through the practices I've outlined for you, you will then be able to awaken your innate power to share with your intimate other, and with *everyone* who crosses your path — your truth, power, happiness, compassion, service, wisdom, and unconditional love at the very highest levels of relationship.

And lastly, remember that all of this is not only possible, but is, in fact, your destiny. Claim it now!

Visit me at:

NoToads.com

OnTheCosmicPorch.com

InspiredTeaching.info

Suggested Reading:

Autobiography of a Yogi by Paramahansa Yogananda

Power versus Force by David R. Hawkins, M.D. Ph.D.

My Stroke of Insight: A Brain Scientist's Personal Journey by Jill Bolte Taylor, Ph.D.

The Power of Intention by Dr. Wayne Dyer

Meditation Techniques:

Self-Realization Fellowship 3880 San Rafael Ave. Los Angeles, CA 90065-3219

(323) 225-2471 yogananda-srf.org

www.ingramcontent.com/pod-product-compliance
Lightning Source LLC
Chambersburg PA
CBHW072246270326
41930CB00010B/2289